CATHOLIC PROPHECY

The Coming Chastisement

Precisions on the Great Disaster

These precisions run from ¶ 12 to ¶ 75. Since they are repeated in many different prophecies, it is not possible to treat them separately. Each of the paragraphs, therefore, may contain one or more of these precisions.

General Events

- Not a two-camp war, but a multi-sided war.
- Not a war only, but a world-wide revolution as well.
- Not simply a man-made holocaust, but also a God-sent chastisement, accompanied by cosmic disturbances.
- To last about four years.

Particular Events

The whole world will be involved in the fighting. A unique feature is the internal disintegration of the Western democracies and the invasion of Western Europe by Arab forces.

The roles of the U.S.A. and U.S.S.R. are not clear in the beginning. The U.S.A. may be involved in the Far-East or at home or both. The U.S.S.R. may want to keep out of the fray at first, while abetting the Arab world, or may be involved in Siberia.

Civil wars rage in Western Europe. The Church is persecuted; the Pope leaves Rome and dies in exile; an anti-pope is installed in Rome; the Catholic Church is split, leaderless and completely disorganized. Communism is victorious. The Mohammedans invade Europe and commit innumerable atrocities.

In the West, however, Christians rally around an unexpected leader, an army officer of royal blood, but their chances seem very slim.

The natural disturbances begin: floods, droughts, famines.

A comet approaches the earth: Whole mountains split open; huge tidal waves swallow up low-lying lands; stones fall from the sky; a deadly fog or gas poisons the atmosphere; a prolonged darkness envelops the earth. Two-thirds or three-fourths of the human race is wiped out.

The powers of evil are shattered. The Christian Prince leads his growing army to battle and wins victory upon victory. In West Germany he crushes a Germano-Russian Army. Communism collapses everywhere. The Mohammedans are thrown back to the sea. The war is carried to Africa and the Middle East, where the Arab Power is dealt a deadly blow. At this stage, if not earlier, U.S. troops come to the assistance of Western Europe.

Russia and China are converted to Catholicism, as also the Mohammedans. All non-Catholics return to Mother Church. A holy Pope is elected; he shows great firmness; and he restores all the former disciplines in the Church.

All the nations of Western Europe unite and form a new Roman Empire, and accept as their emperor the great Christian Prince, chosen by God, who works hand-in-hand with the holy Pope. The triumph of the Catholic Church is universal.

The whole world enjoys a period of complete peace and unprecedented prosperity in mutual love and respect among people and nations.

This great peace will last until the coming of Antichrist.

CATHOLIC PROPHECY

THE COMING CHASTISEMENT

by

Yves Dupont

And they did not understand
Until the flood came and
Swept them all away.
(Matt. 24:39)

TAN BOOKS AND PUBLISHERS, INC.
P.O. Box 424
Rockford, Illinois 61105

ISBN: 0-89555-015-6

Printed and bound in the United States of America.

TAN BOOKS AND PUBLISHERS, INC.
P. O. Box 424
Rockford, Illinois 61105

Table of Contents

Publisher's Preface

A number of reasons exist for publishing this volume of prophecies and commentaries. First of all, one hears much at the present time about our being in the Great Apostasy foretold by St. Paul (2 *Thes.* 2:3). The author's research indicates this is most likely *not* the case. Secondly, one also hears much about our being in the time of Antichrist. The prophecies of this book, however, indicate that a number of events have yet to be fulfilled before his coming. (This is not to deny the time of Antichrist could indeed be *close*.) Thirdly, if future events develop according to these prophecies, it will be just one more proof the Catholic Church is the one, true Church of God. Fourthly, if these prophecies are true, then the world — each and every one of us — needs more than ever to repent, pray and do penance. So, this book is implicitly *a call to spiritual warfare* against the forces of hell let loose on earth. Fifthly, historic developments do in fact indicate we have already entered the period foretold by these prophecies. And finally, as the author mentions, there are many, many other prophecies which substantiate those in this book; thus, the number, content, and reinforcement of these predictions is such to demand in justice, so to speak, that they be disseminated. For these prophecies help us to understand what is wrong with our world; it has rejected Christ and His divine counsels and has adopted instead erroneous human counsels suggested by the very *enemies* of Christ. And these prophecies help us know what we can do about our times — pray and consecrate our lives to God, and prepare ourselves for the coming events. May this little volume reach and enlighten many people, and may it help fulfill the will of Our Lord Jesus Christ in the work of saving souls.

Thomas A. Nelson
1970

About The Author

Yves Dupont was born in 1922 at Paris, where he spent his childhood. He was educated at the Collège de Royan on the southwest coast of France north of Bordeaux. In early 1941, shortly after the outbreak of war, he joined the French Colonial Army in North Africa, where he became a practicing Catholic, and later fought alongside the American Army there, in Italy, and in France and Germany. During the bitter winter of 1944 he received the *Croix de Guerre* in Alsace. After the War, he lived several years in Paris and then left France for Australia, where he currently lives with his wife of English birth and their four children.

In 1938 at the age of 16, the author read his first book of prophecy; it predicted the death of Pope Pius XI for the spring of 1939. When this prediction came about, he decided to investigate prophecy more thoroughly. Two years later, at the age of 18 and while still in school, he wrote a prophetical "summary." That summary stated: "The war will soon break out. France will be defeated. The Nazis will pitch their tents on the banks of the River Loire." The master on duty that evening found him writing this, read it, and commented, "My young fellow, don't waste your time with such nonsense." "The French people," Mr. Dupont reminisces, "from the Prime Minister down to the school janitor, were supremely confident that the 'powerful' French Army would dispose of Hitler within a few months if he were rash enough to go to war. But the war broke out six months later. After a few months of the 'phony' war (the war of skirmishes), the Nazis struck in May 1940, and the French Army was defeated in three weeks, completely destroyed in six. Not only did the Nazis reach the Loire, they even went farther down, to the Garonne. Four long years of occupation had begun."

"After the War, I resumed my prophetical studies. By then, I was aware that prophecies have a far deeper significance than a mere listing of events to come. I could see too that the post-war political scene showed the same errors and faults which had been responsible for the rise of Hitler." *Les Derniers Jours des Derniers Temps (The Last Days of the Last Times),* the author's first book on prophecy, was published in Paris in 1959, and the second one, a *pro manuscripto* book, in Belgium in 1962. At Melbourne in 1962 he also began publishing *World Trends,* a Catholic quarterly of comment on events in the Church and in the political and social arenas (his popular article "Garabandal" has been republished from *World Trends* by TAN Books and Publishers). "My observations of the proceedings of Vatican II prompted me to express fears and misgivings for the future of the Church." Rereading those early issues of *World Trends,* one is profoundly impressed by the accuracy of Mr. Dupont's analyses at that time. Indeed, his prognostications of 1962 to 1965 are as fresh and vigorous today as they were then. At a time of "surface calm" in the Church, many of his readers were incredulous at his predictions of trouble and dissention soon to come. He believes the fears of that time have now been vindicated and the Church is split. He believes also that we are entering the period predicted by the prophecies in this book.

In presenting the present volume, Mr. Dupont states that he has enough material for four such books. The response this one receives will determine his authoring others.

INTRODUCTION

Private and Public Prophecies

Private revelations (i.e. apparitions and locutions with or without prophecies) are those which have been recorded since the days of Christ. Revelations which were recorded up to the days of Christ are known as public, biblical, or scriptural revelations.

Private revelations do not belong to the deposit of faith and, as such, are not binding upon our faith. Nevertheless, it is an indisputable fact that Almighty God often speaks to His servants in an unmistakable manner. Many Catholic devotions are based solely on private revelations: the Rosary, the Sacred Heart, and the Scapular are cases in point. More recently, devotion to Our Lady of Fatima was accepted and encouraged by the Church. There is ample evidence that revelations have taken place throughout the centuries right up to the present time, and it is likely that some are taking place at this very moment.

The Importance of Prophecies

Saint Paul said: "Aim at charity, yet strive after the spiritual gifts, but especially that you may prophesy. He who prophesies speaks to men for edification and encouragement and consolation. Now, I should like you all to speak in tongues, but still more to prophesy; for he who prophesies is greater than he who speaks in tongues." (1 *Cor.* 14:1,3,5)

Indeed, prophecies are for our edification: They cast a light on many problems; they warn us against errors; they prepare us for dangers to come; and they are a manifestation of the power of God. At the same time, they are an encouragement and a consolation. The current crisis in the Church and in the world was predicted long ago, but the final victory of the Christian forces is also predicted; this is an encouragement and a consolation.

The Reformation in the 16th century, the so-called Age of Enlightenment in the 18th, and the rise of democracy in the 20th, were all predicted and called "deadly errors." The Enlightenment, as a matter of fact, was described as the beginning of an age of spiritual darkness; this is self-evident today. The rise of popular power (sometimes called "the Fourth Estate" in the prophecies) was defined as being against the natural order willed by God, and it was said that it would end in chaos, anarchy, and bloodshed. We are fast approaching that stage; there is now throughout the world a general revolt against authority that leaves little doubt as to the outcome.

Thus, what the vast majority of people today regard as their most cherished values was denounced as errors. It is quite possible that many of us have been so influenced by modern ideas that we may find it difficult to accept what these prophecies say. But this is another question, for the prophecies do not ask for our assent; they simply warn us and describe events which, once they have come to pass, will *force* our assent. Yes, we are free to *reject* the prophecies, but we do not possess the *right* to do so. Freedom is not a right, it is a duty or, more accurately, it is a faculty of our make-up which implies a duty. We possess the faculty to choose between good and evil, between truth and error, between God and Satan — a privilege which the lower animals do not possess, but our duty is to choose God, truth, and goodness. The modern concept of freedom-is-a-right is a distortion of Catholic truth.

The Basis of This Study

I have studied several hundred of these prophecies over the last thirty years or so; I have written books about them. These books, in turn, have resulted in my getting into touch with people whom I would never have heard from otherwise. Thus, I came to receive the unpublished manuscripts of a saintly French priest who died shortly afterwards; these comprised well over 1,000 pages and contained unprocurable material of immense value together with a scholarly analysis of private prophecies. This holy man was a country priest. I can imagine him in his little village for many years on end spending every evening of his solitary life assembling and analyzing this unique monument of prophetical writings, one of the few typewritten copies of which he finally sent to me.

The material I now possess is indeed monumental, and it would take many books to include it all. But this would not in any case be desirable, as many of these prophecies are repetitive. This is so because God has multiplied His warnings throughout the centuries, in many different countries, to innumerable people, in order that we might all know of the terrible events which are to take place in this, our apocalyptic age.

It is on the basis of this material that I invite you to read this little book.

1

PROPHECIES AND COMMENTARIES

¶ 1. *Teresa Neumann* (1936). "The furies of hell are now set loose. Divine punishment is inevitable."

¶ 2. *St. Columba* (6th century). "Hearken, hearken to what will happen in the latter days of the world! There will be great wars; unjust laws will be enacted; the Church will be despoiled of her property; people will read and write a great deal; but charity and humility will be laughed to scorn, and the common people will believe in false ideas."

¶ 3. *Elizabeth Canori-Mora* (19th century). "Woe to the religious who does not observe his rule! I say the same to the secular clergy and to all people in the world who give themselves to a life of pleasure and who believe in the false maxims of modern ideas."

¶ 4. *Berthe Petit* (1943). "The human race will have to go through a great storm that will sharpen divisions among men and reduce their plans to ashes."

¶ 5. *Brother Louis Rocco* (19th century). "A Great King will arise after a period of terrible wars and persecutions."

¶ 6. *St. Methodius* (4th century). "A day will come when the enemies of Christ will boast of having conquered the whole world. They will say: 'Christians cannot escape now!' But a Great King will arise to fight the enemies of God. He will defeat them, and peace will be given to the world, and the Church will be freed from her anxieties."

¶ 7. *Pius IX* (19th century). "There will be a great prodigy which will fill the world with awe. But this prodigy will be preceded by the triumph of a revolution during which the Church will go through ordeals that are beyond description."

¶ 8. *Mélanie Calvat* (The Seeress of La Salette, 19th century) "After a frightful war a Great King will arise and his reign will be marked by a wonderful peace and a great religious revival."

¶ 9. *St. Cataldus* (5th century). "The Great King will wage war until the age of forty. He will assemble great armies, and hurl back the tyrants out of his empire."

¶ 10. *Fr. Souffrand* (19th century). "During the reign of the Great King, the noblest virtues will be practised throughout the world, and the land will yield abundant crops."

¶ 11. *Rudolph Gekner* (17th century). "A Great Prince of the North with a most powerful army will traverse all Europe, uproot all the republics, and defeat all the rebels. His sword moved by divine power will most valiantly defend the Church of Jesus Christ."

Comment: These are but a few excerpts given to you as an introduction. Many more need to be read and carefully collated before the general outline of events can take form and before many seemingly indifferent phrases can assume a deeper significance. I did that job many years ago; so, I can, even now, add a few useful comments to the above passages.

St. Columba's prophecy has already come to pass: We have had two world wars so far; unjust laws have been enacted in every country; the Church lost her property in 1870; the development of the printing press has caused people to read and write a great deal, something which was impossible for anyone but a saint to visualize in the 6th century; charity and humility are now scoffed at, and people believe in the false human messianism which arose during the Renaissance in intellectual quarters, and which has spread among the common people from the 18th Century onwards. But more of this later; we shall soon see what this false human messianism involves in practical terms. We shall see, also, how and why it must be regarded as the cause of the coming disaster. Thus, this little phrase jotted down as if in passing by St. Columba will assume a deeper significance.

Elizabeth Canori-Mora, too, alludes to the "false maxims of modern ideas." Many other private prophecies do so and some in great detail; we shall see some of them.

Berthe Petit announces the great disaster that will cause the almost total collapse of modern civilization. Br. Louis Rocco foretells the Great King who is to rule over Europe and extend his moral influence throughout the whole world during the period of peace which will follow the great disaster.

St. Methodius was one of the earliest prophets of the Christian era to foresee the victory of Communism. He did not name Communism, but correlations with other prophecies will make this clear. Many other prophecies say that the victory of

Communism will seem so certain that they, the Communists, will throw up their caps and shout about their triumph. At that very moment a cosmic phenomenon will take place, and help the designs of the future King's small army (it is only later that his army will grow to be very large). This most Christian prince will reduce the Communists to a rabble.

Pius IX alludes to the same episode, although in different terms: he sees the cosmic phenomenon that will follow the triumph of the Communist revolution.

Mélanie Calvat also foretells the rise of the Great King, the wonderful period of peace, and the religious revival which is to follow. So does St. Cataldus in the 5th century and, again, Fr. Souffrand in the 19th century.

Rudolph Gekner confirms all the above predictions and adds that this King will "uproot all republics." Countless prophecies develop this point, saying that this King will herald a new social and political order in which authority will be hierarchical and descending, instead of popular and ascending. This is an aspect of political philosophy to which we shall have occasion to return.

¶ 12. *St. Malachy* (12th century). "Ireland will suffer English oppression for a week of centuries, but will preserve her fidelity to God and His Church. At the end of that time she will be delivered, and the English in turn must suffer severe chastisement. Ireland, however, will be instrumental in bringing back the English to the unity of Faith."

Comment: The authenticity of older prophecies is sometimes open to question. The above has been challenged. On the other hand, many reliable authors regard it as genuine, and it is indeed a striking prophecy in many respects: In the 12th century, England had just begun the conquest of Ireland, but she was still Catholic. The persecutions did not start until the 16th or 17th century. Despite these ferocious persecutions, Ireland preserved her Faith. The liberation has come in stages: World War I, independence within the British Empire; World War II, complete independence. Thus, Ireland was under British rule for seven centuries. It is likely that the severe chastisements which England will soon suffer, according to other prochecies, will be the prelude to her return to the Catholic Faith.

¶ 13. *St. Thomas a'Becket* (12th century). "A knight shall come from the West. He shall capture Milan, Lombardy, and the three Crowns. He shall then sail to Cyrprus and Fama-goste and land at Jaffa, and reach Christ's grave where he will fight. Wars and wonders shall befall till the people believe in Christ toward the end of the world."

Comment: As it stands this prophecy is *abstruse.* However, it confirms what is known from more specific prophecies: The Knight is the great Christian King who will be chosen by God to destroy Communism and to whom the U.S.A. will lend its material power. He will fight first in France and in Germany, then in Italy, and he will liberate the Vatican ("Three Crowns" equals the Tiara). He will then sail to Palestine to restore Christianity there. Many prophecies confirm this, how-ever incredible it may now sound.

¶ 14. *St. Hildegard* (12th century). "The time is coming when princes and peoples will reject the authority of the Pope. Some countries will prefer their own Church rulers to the Pope. The German Empire will be divided. Church property will be secularized. Priests will be persecuted. Toward the end of the world mankind will be purified through sufferings. This will be true especially of the clergy who will be robbed of all property."

Comment: This prophecy is already partly fulfilled: many countries became protestant in the 16th century, and the Ger-man Empire was divided as a result.

¶ 15. *St. Hildegard* (Continuation). "A powerful wind will rise in the north carrying heavy fog and the densest of dust by divine command, and it will fill their throats and eyes so that they will cease their savagery and be stricken with a great fear. Before the comet comes, many nations, the good ex-cepted, will be scourged by want and famine. The great nation in the ocean that is inhabited by people of different tribes and descent will be devastated by an [*sic.*] earthquake, storm, and tidal wave. It will be divided and, in great part, submerged. That nation will also have many misfortunes at sea and lose its colonies. By its tremendous pressure the comet will force much out of the ocean and flood many countries, causing much want and many plagues. All coastal cities will live in fear, and many of them will be destroyed by tidal waves, and most living creatures will be killed, and even those who escape will die from horrible diseases. For in none of those cities does a person live according to the laws of God.

"Peace will return to the world when the white flower again takes possession of the throne of France. During this period of peace, people will be forbidden to carry weapons, and iron will be used only for making agricultural implements and tools. Also during this period, the land will be very productive, and many Jews, heathens, and heretics will join the Church."

Comment: Many more prophecies mention wind of such velocity and fog and dust of such thickness that men will be forced to stop killing each other. This natural disaster will cause much loss of life and great destruction. After the failure of harvests, many people will starve to death, and their unburied bodies will cause terrible epidemics. The nation of "many tribes" in the ocean does not seem to be America. In fact, another prophecy names England, a former great colonial power, which was also made up of many different tribes in the beginning. The "White Flower" is the Lily, the symbol of French Monarchy. The Great King will rule over the whole of Western Europe. His will be the new Roman Empire at the end of which, according to many Fathers of the Church, will come the last persecutions of Antichrist. Although St. Hildegard was a German Saint, she mentions France in particular. Why? Because France, for better or for worse has always had a great influence on world affairs. France poisoned the whole world with the deadly doctrines of her 18th-century philosophers, Rousseau and Voltaire in particular. The French Revolution marked the triumph of these philosophers' ideas, which took root first in America, then throughout Europe in the wake of Napoleon's victorious armies. From Europe, they spread throughout the world in the ensuing colonial period. The social and political institutions of the whole world — including Communism — are the logical development of those ideas. It is fitting, therefore, that the Counter-Revolution should start in France too. And, indeed, it is in France that the Great King, according to all prophecies, will begin his work.

¶ 16. *Monk Adso* (10th century). "Some of our Teachers say that a King of the Franks will possess the entire Roman Empire. He will be the greatest and the last of all Monarchs. After having wisely governed his kingdom, he will go in the end to Jerusalem and will lay down his sceptre and his crown upon the Mount of Olives. Immediately afterwards, Antichrist will come."

Comment: The Great King will be of Frankish descent, although his actual nationality is uncertain. Inter-marriage between the various royal families of Europe makes it possible for virtually every prince to claim Frankish ancestry.

It seems that he will travel twice to Jerusalem, once at the beginning of his reign to reassert the right of the Christians, and again at the end to fight Israel, which by then, will have grown powerful under the rising Antichrist. The mention of his laying down his sceptre and crown, coupled with that of Antichrist, seems to indicate that he will be defeated and killed by the Anti-Christians. This interpretation is confirmed by other prochecies. Thus will end the period of complete peace and prosperity which is to follow the coming disaster. And after this the End of the World, which is to mark the triumph of righteousness, and the reward of the elect will be quite close.

¶ 17. *St. Edward* (11th century). "The extreme corruption and wickedness of the English nation has provoked the just anger of God. When malice has reached the fullness of its measure, God will, in His wrath, send to the English people evil spirits who will punish and afflict them with severity by separating the green tree from its parent stem the length of three furlongs. But at last this same tree, through the compassionate mercy of God and without any national assistance, shall return to its original root, reflourish, and bear abundant fruit."

Comment: Here again we see that the Anglican schism was predicted centuries before its actual occurrence. But St. Edward, the King of the Anglo-Saxons, was off the mark concerning the duration of the schism — unless a furlong is not meant to be a century, or unless this prophecy was tampered with at some time in the past. This is not rare with older prophecies; we are on much firmer ground with the many 19th-Century prophecies, which we also possess. It is to be noted, too, that there was no English nation as such in the 11th Century, but only a kingdom of the Angles and Saxons. This discrepancy, however, may be due to a mis-transcription.

¶ 18. *St. Malachy* (12th century). (Following is a list of the last Popes according to a prophecy attributed to St. Malachy. Each Pope is designated by a short motto. Rejected as spurious by some Catholic commentators (including Dr. Rumble of Sydney), this prophecy has been accepted by many other scholars as genuine. In any case, it has given fitting descriptions of every Pope since the 16th century, when it was discovered. The following are the last twelve mottoes:

Crux de Cruce ("Cross from a Cross"). Pius IX, the Pope who had to bear the Cross of the Italian Revolution backed up by the House of Savoy, the Coat of Arms of which features a Cross.

Lumen in Coelo ("Light in the Heaven"). Leo XIII, the Pope coming from the Pecci family whose coat of arms featured a comet. He was also a brilliant writer ("light") for the Church (heaven).

Ignis Ardens ("Burning Fire"). St. Pius X. World War I ("burning fire") broke out on the 11th Anniversary of his election. He was also "on fire" with zeal and was canonized 40 years after his death.

Religio Depopulata ("Christendom depopulated"). Benedict XV, the Pope of World War I.

Fides Intrepida ("Fearless Faith"). Pius XI, the Pope of the Propagation of the Faith.

Pastor Angelicus ("Angelic Shepherd"). Pius XII, a Pope of unquestioned holiness.

Pastor et Nauta ("Shepherd and Sailor"). John XXIII, mostly concerned with pastoral problems, this Pope came from Venice, the Sailors' city. He also set the Church on a "new" course with his *aggiornamento*.

Flos Florum ("Flower of Flowers"). Paul VI. Uncertain significance: the flower of flowers is the lily which the Pope's coat of arms is said to feature, but it may also mean martyrdom.

De Mediatate Lunae ("From the Midst of the Moon," often translated, "From the Half of the Moon"). The biblical symbolism of the "moon" is "the worldly kingdom" or the "temporal order." This Pope may therefore be elected from the midst of cardinals who are mainly influenced by worldly ideas (social gospel, etc.), or he may be elected at a time when the forces of Satan (the "Prince of this World") have virtual control of the entire earth via their secret government, possibly even influencing the papal election, so that an agent of the world antichrist government is elected Pope. Still another explanation is that he will be a bad Pope, himself influenced and dominated by worldly ideas, and thus do great havoc to the Church. Finally, this enigmatic formula may indicate that during his reign, the Moslem world (the crescent or "half moon") will gain ascendancy and possibly even attack Europe, as Monk Hilarion's prophecy, below, would indicate.

De Labore Solis ("Of the Labour of the Sun"). This is the same symbol as that of *Apocalype* 12:1-5, of a woman clothed with the sun in labor to give birth to a son, who subsequently rules the earth with "a rod of iron." H. B. Kramer, interpreting the *Apocalypse* in his *Book of Destiny*, maintains this figure represents a highly disputed papal election (dispute = labor; woman = Church; sun = the light of divine truth).

De Gloria Olivae ("Of the Glory of the Olive Tree"). May refer to the glorious period of peace under the Great King (wherein the Church is consoled and succored as with the balm of the olive), but it may also refer to the rising power of Israel (the Olive).

Petrus Romanus ("Peter the Roman"). The last Pope, whose name will probably be Peter II. This motto is accompanied by a description referring to the last persecutions and to the last judgment.

¶ 19. *Monk Hilarion* (15th century). "Before the Christian churches are reunited and renovated, God will send the Eagle who will travel to Rome and bring much happiness and good. The Holy Man will bring peace between the clergy and the Eagle, and his reign will last for four years. After his death God will send three men who are rich in wisdom and virtue. They will spread Christianity everywhere. There will be one flock, one shepherd, one faith, one law, one life, and one baptism throughout the world.

"The people of the peninsula of Europe will suffer by needless wars until the Holy Man comes. The Lion will come from a high mountain in the enlightened nation. Then will the people of the half-moon of the tribe of Agar overrun many nations towards midnight and commit many atrocities. They will stay three years destroying everything. Yet, in the third year, will one of the unconquerable Eagles who reigns over the enlightened nation between the Rhine and the North sea, with a great army meet them by the mouth of the River Rhine and, in a fearful battle, almost entirely annihilate them."

Comment: This prophecy contains much symbolism and is anything but clear. A few details, however, stand out, and with correlations drawn from other prophecies, it is possible to suggest a tentative explanation: the Eagle, who is also often called the Lion, is the Great King, at first disliked by the Clergy, but who will be supported by the Pope. Of this Pope it is said elsewhere that he will be very holy (hence: "Holy Man"), yet very firm (will rule with "a rod of iron"). He will restore the former disciplines (apparently abolished by a previous Pope), and he will censure the bishops who refuse to submit to his rule. It is under his leadership that the Church will be reborn. He will reign only four years, and three more Popes are to follow him. Then, the scriptural prophecy "one flock, one pope, one faith" will be fulfilled.

Before the reign of the Holy Man, however, Europe — and Italy in particular — will suffer greatly through wars. The Mohammedans will take advantage of the complete anarchy in Europe and invade the land (a great many prophecies say so). But they will eventually be thrown back into the sea by the Great King who comes from the Ardennes, in Belgium (The Ardennes is the cradle of the Capetian Royal family).

¶ 20.1 *Old English Prophecy*   (On a tombstone at the Kirby cemetery, Essex).

> When pictures look alive, with movements free,
>   (T.V. and movies)
> When ships like fish swim beneath the sea,
>   (Submarines)
> When men outstripping birds can soar the sky,
>   (Jets and rockets)
> Then half the world deep drenched in blood shall die.

¶ 20.2

> In Germany begins a dance,

> Which passeth through Italy, Spain and France.
> But England shall pay the piper.

(A 20th-century German prophecy says exactly the same thing: strife will start in Germany, spread to Italy, France and Spain, but England will suffer most.)
¶ 20.3

> When Our Lady shall lie on Our Lord's lap,
> Then England will meet with a strange mishap.

(This seems to refer to a Feast of Our Lady occurring between two Feasts of Our Lord, perhaps a Feast of Mary on Easter Saturday by opposition to Good Friday when Our Lord rested on Mary's lap after the Crucifixion)

¶ 21. *St. Pius X* (20th century). "I saw one of my successors taking to flight over the bodies of his brethren. He will take refuge in disguise somewhere; and after a short retirement he will die a cruel death. The present wickedness of the world is only the beginning of the sorrows which must take place before the end of the world."

¶ 22. *Pius XII* (20th century). "We believe that the present hour is a dread phase of the events foretold by Christ. It seems that darkness is about to fall on the world. Humanity is in the grip of a supreme crisis."

Comment: After quoting St. Pius X and Pius XII, however, it is of some interest to contrast what John XXIII said at the opening of the Second Council of the Vatican:

"We feel we must disagree with those prophets of gloom, who are always forecasting disaster, as though the end of the world was at hand.

"In the present order of things, Divine Providence is leading us to a new order of human relations which, by men's own efforts and even beyond their very expectations, are directed towards the fulfilment of God's superior and inscrutable designs. And everything, even human differences, leads to the greater good of the Church."

Comment: On the strength of this declaration we cannot but observe that John XXIII disagreed with St. Pius X and Pius XII, as well as with all the holy souls who have been granted private revelations. Further, we are now to believe that men's efforts will, automatically so to speak, bring about the fulfilment of God's designs, even though men's efforts today are not conspicuously directed to the greater glory of God. I cannot help recalling one of the pet theses of Teilhard de Chardin (whose books were condemned by the Holy Office) which equated human progress (technological or otherwise) with spiritual development. The last sentence of the above passage further aggravates this piece of Teilhardian humanism by claiming that even differenecs lead to the greater good of the Church. May I suggest that since 1962, when this address was given, the growing differences within the Catholic Church do not appear to have done a lot of good! Karl Marx, to be sure, taught that conflicts and differences always work for the good of the cause concerned, but we were not quite prepared to hear this from the mouth of a Pope. In justice to good Pope John, however, I must add that this opening address was written for him by the then Cardinal Montini.

Let us go back to the safer ground of our prophecies. As you will see in due course, many tell us that men's present efforts will lead the world to chaos and destruction. Biblical prophecies, too, warn us that the end will be close when men worship the work of their own hands — which is precisely the case today when machines and motor-cars are more important than children, when higher production targets are boldly promoted along with abortion laws.

¶ 23. *Bishop Christianos Ageda* (12th century). "In the 20th century there will be wars and fury which will last a long time; whole provinces shall be emptied of their inhabitants, and kingdoms shall be thrown into confusion. In many places the land shall be left untilled, and there shall be great slaughters of the upper class. The right hand of the world shall fear the left, and the north shall prevail over the south."

¶ 24. *St. John of the Cleft Rock* (14th century). "It is said that twenty centuries after the Incarnation of the Word, the Beast in its turn shall become man. About the year 2000 A.D., Antichrist will reveal himself to the world."

¶ 25. *Sister Bouquillion* (19th century). "The beginning of the end shall not come in the 19th century, but in the 20th for sure."

¶ 26. *Old Saxon Prophecy*. "The seven-headed city, now

more admirable than Jerusalem, shall be a place more desolate than Jerusalem. The Dog shall enter Germany but shall afterwards forsake his master and choose for himself a new man, whereby Scripture shall be fulfilled. This Dog shall signify the Turk which shall forsake his Mohammed and choose unto him the name Christian, which is a sign the day of doom is at hand, when all the earth is subject unto God, or that all people acknowledge one only God. The Fleur-de-Lys (lily) and France shall live long at variance, but at last agree. Then shall the clear Word spring forth and flourish throughout the world.

"But after all these things the end of the world shall approach, and there shall be heavy and pitiful days."

Comment: The seven-headed city is probably Rome (*septicolis* — seven hills). Other prophecies predict that it will be looted and destroyed by the Mohammedans, who will go as far as Germany where, as we have seen, they will be defeated by the Great King. The King will cross the seas and carry the war into Arab lands, which will eventually bring about the conversion of the Mohammedans. France will be without a monarchy for a long time, but it will be finally restored and, as a result, French thinkers will spread words of truth and wisdom (instead of errors and follies). All these things will take place during the reign of the Great European and Christian King, shortly before the coming of Antichrist and the end of the world (See previous prophecies in this respect).

¶ 27. *Old German Prophecy.* "When the world becomes godless, revolutions will break out against kings. Fathers will fight their sons, and the sons their fathers. The doctrine will be perverted, and they will try to overthrow the Catholic Church. Men will be pleasure-loving. A terrible war will find the North fighting the South. The South will be led by a Prince wearing a white coat with a cross on the front; he will be lame afoot. He will gather his forces at Bremen for Mass. Then he will lead them into battle beyond Woerl near the birch-tree country (Westphalia). After a terrible battle at a brook running eastwards near Berdberg and Sondern, the South will be victorious.

Comment: This prophecy does not contradict Bishop Ageda's quoted earlier. For the North will be victorious at first (See St. Methodius and Pius IX above). Note, too, the prediction about the perversion of doctrine in the Catholic Church, which is the case today, especially since the introduction of the New Order of the Mass *(Novus Ordo Missae)* which has given official status to earlier anti-Catholic trends. Again, the overthrow of the Catholic Church has now become a very real threat with the existence of IDO-C to which many priests belong.

This prophecy mentions also the Prince who will be "lame afoot." He is none other than the Great King to-be. His lameness is also referred to by Sister Anne Catherine Emmerich in a 19th-century prophecy which we shall see later. This Prince, or King, whose arrival is foretold in a large number of prophecies, will engage the enemy although his forces will be greatly outnumbered. He will first take his troops to Mass and, with the help of God, he will throw back the enemy. The battle described above is that of the "Birch-tree," well known by all students of private prophecies and described in many prophecies. It will be fought mainly against Russian and East German troops. The King's troops will be mainly made up of Spanish, Italian, Austrian and French soldiers. All these precisions may well seem incredible, but that is what the prophecies say. The reader may not believe it all (but, please, spare me the disgrace of thinking that I am making up stories, for I am only relating what I have read).

The American reader may wonder why American troops have nowhere been mentioned so far. Indeed, except for a few prophecies mentioning rather vaguely some overseas soldiers who may or may not be Americans, the presence of the U.S.A. in Western Europe is nowhere clearly indicated in the hagiographical prophecies that I know of. There is some reason to believe that the U.S.A. will have its hands full in the Far-East, and will also have to deal with serious civil strife at home. This may explain why the U.S.A. will not intervene in Western Europe at the beginning. It must also be borne in mind that the coming disaster (which I purposely do not call World War III) is not likely to start with a conventional foreign invasion, but rather internally through civil war and revolution. In this case, American intervention would be very unlikely indeed.

Of all the prophecies that I know, there is only one which refers clearly enough to the U.S.A., and it is a non-hagiographical prophecy. In one particular passage, this 16th-century prophecy goes as far as naming the U.S.A. — "Americh." However, I shall not quote that passage because, apart from the word "Americh" (pronounced "Amerik"), it is quite unintelligible. But I shall quote others which, in my opinion, make it clear that the U.S.A. will intervene in the latter half of the Great Disaster which, by then, will have developed into a war properly so-called.

Now, one reason I do not call the Great Disaster "World War III" is that (as said before) it will not start as a war, but rather as civil disturbance and revolution throughout Western Europe. It may be triggered by a limited military intervention (such as East Germany's taking over West Berlin) but it will go no further. My main reason, however, for not calling the Great Disaster "World War III" is the knowledge that the appalling loss of life throughout the world will be caused, not by human weapons, including nuclear ones, but by natural disturbances of unprecedented severity. But more of this later.

¶ 28. *Magdeburg Chronicle.* "Of the blood of the Emperor Charles the Great and of the Kings of France shall arise an Emperor named Charles, who shall rule in Europe, by whom the decayed Estate of the Church shall be reformed and the ancient glory of the Empire restored."

Comment: The Bible says that we do not know "either the hour or the day" when Christ will come again. Christ, however, gave us a number of indications in order to enable us to determine the approximate period. The Fathers and the Doctors of the Church wrote at length on these proximate signs. The return of the Jews to their land is one of them. The end of the Roman Empire is another. Thus, all those private prophecies which announce the restoration of the Empire, to be followed by Antichrist, are elaborating on, but adding nothing new to the general outline of events recorded in the Bible.

¶ 29. *Abbot Joachin Merlin* (13th century). "After many long sufferings endured by Christians, and after too great an effusion of innocent blood, the Lord shall give peace and happiness to the desolated nations. A remarkable Pope will be seated on the pontifical Throne under the special protection of the Angels. Holy and full of gentleness, he shall undo all wrong; he shall recover the Estate of the Church, and reunite the exiled temporal powers. He shall be revered by everybody, and shall recover the Kingdom of Jerusalem. He shall reunite the Eastern and the Western Churches. The sanctity of this beneficent Pontiff will be so great that the highest potentates shall bow down in his presence. All men will return to the primitive Church, and there shall be only one Pastor, one Law, one Master — humble, modest, and fearing God.

"Before being firmly and solidly established in the Holy See, however, there will be countless wars and violent conflicts during which the sacred Throne will be shaken. But through the favour of divine mercy, moved by the prayers of the faithful, everything will succeed so well that they shall be able to sing hymns of thanksgiving to the glory of the Lord. In order to obtain these happy results, having need of a powerful temporal assistance, the Holy Pontiff will ask for the collaboration of the generous Monarch of France."

Comment: All this talk about Kings, Thrones and Kingdoms may well seem so hopelessly out-of-date that the reader may be tempted to dismiss all these prophecies as rank nonsense. I am well aware of this; we have all been brought up in the belief that popular forms of government mean progress, and that democracy and progress are inseparable. Under those premises, therefore, a return to non-popular forms of government, it is thought, must needs mean a return to the Dark Ages. But we should not be too optimistic in our assessment of the modern world. The history of past civilization shows that governments have been in the main non-popular, and no one will deny that some of the extinct civilizations reached very high standards indeed. Reviewing past civilizations in a previous book which I published in the French language, I gave evidence that these periods enjoyed comparative stability. Wars, there were, of course, but these wars did not involve the *whole* nation and the *whole* people as they now do, but only the regular armies of professional soldiers. In point of fact, it was Napoleon I who first introduced compulsory conscription on a large scale, thus forcing other European nations to follow suit. Therefore, the myth of "popular sovereignty" soon gave rise to the very real curse of popular involvement in warfare. History further shows that periods of popular governments were also periods of decay and degeneracy and that they brought to an end, in chaos and anarchy, the brilliant civilizations I have just referred to. These are lessons we should not forget; and, if we do not forget them, it might help us to re-assess the worth of the teachings imparted to us in our school-days regarding modern "progress" — teachings which followed the guidelines of a certain Judeo-Masonic philosophy.

Now, the point I should like to stress is this: the coming disaster will be of such magnitude that our whole civilization would be destroyed were it not for the presence of the Church. *It is the Church that will save civilization.* And the *totality* of the errors of our modern age will be exposed and rejected by those who survive. This explains the sudden return to non-popular forms of government.

¶ 30. *John of Vatiguerro* (13th century). "Spoilation, pillaging, and devastation of that most famous city which is the capital and mistress of France will take place when the Church and the world are grievously troubled. The Pope will change his residence and the Church will not be defended for twenty-five months or more because, during all that time, there will be no Pope in Rome, no emperor and no ruler in France. But, after this, a young captive prince shall recover the Crown of the Lilies and shall extend his dominions all over the world.

"After many tribulations, a Pope shall be elected out of those who survived the persecutions. By his sanctity he will reform the clergy, and the whole world shall venerate the Church for her sanctity, virtue, and perfection."

Comment: This is the first of many references to the destruction of Paris, to take place when the Church and the world are in deep ferment. This is also the first of many references to the Pope's exile and vacancy of the Holy See. France will be in the throes of a murderous civil war, but she will be saved by the Prince — the Great King to-be.

A word of caution here: although the Prince will be crowned King of France, and although he will "extend his dominions all over the world," this must not be understood as meaning that France will conquer the whole world — for two different reasons: first, because this King will also be crowned

King of other European countries (he may, but need not be French). He will be, in fact, Emperor of Europe, and it is as such that he will extend his dominions all over the world Second, because "all over the world" does not mean "over the *whole* world." It would be extravagant to assume that the European Emperor would want to dominate the whole white race in Europe, Africa, America and Australia. It would mean that he will dominate and guide various primitive nations in certain parts of the world and exert strong influence upon the others.

¶ 31. *John of the Cleft Rock* (14th century).   "Towards the end of the world, tyrants and hostile mobs will rob the Church and the clergy of all their possessions and will afflict and martyr them. Those who heap the most abuse upon them will be held in high esteem.

"The clergy cannot escape these persecutions, but, because of them, all the servants of the Church will be forced to lead an apostolic life.

"At that time, the Pope with his cardinals will have to flee Rome in tragic circumstances to a place where they will be unknown. The Pope will die a cruel death in his exile. The sufferings of the Church will be much greater than at any previous time in her history. But God will raise a holy Pope, and the Angels will rejoice. Enlightened by God, this man will rebuild almost the whole world through his holiness. He will lead everyone to the true Faith. Everywhere, the fear of God, virtue, and good morals will prevail. He will lead all erring sheep back to the fold, and there shall be one faith, one law, one rule of life, and one baptism on earth. All men will love each other and do good, and all quarrels and wars will cease."

¶ 32. *St. Vincent Ferrer* (15th century).   "Armies from the West, East, and North will fight together in Italy, and the Eagle shall capture the false king, and all things shall be made obedient unto him, and there shall be a new reformation in the world.

"In the days of peace that are to come after the desolation of revolutions and wars — before the end of the world — Christians will become so lax in their religion that they will refuse the sacrament of Confirmation, saying that it is unnecessary. And when the false prophet, the precursor of Antichrist, comes, all who are not confirmed will apostatize, while those who are confirmed will stand fast in their faith, and only a few will renounce Christ."

Comment: From a complete study of prophecies it is almost certain that there will be two distinct periods of wars: one to come soon, which will be followed by a period of peace and prosperity; and another to follow the period of peace, and which will be that of Antichrist. The latter period will in turn be followed by the triumph of the Church and by another period of peace of unknown duration. The Gospel, too, seems to confirm that there will be two different periods: the beginning of the end, and the end proper, with an intervening respite.

¶ 33. *Nicholas of Fluh* (15th century).   "The Church will be punished because the majority of her members, high and low, will become so perverted. The Church will sink deeper and deeper until she will at last seem to be extinguished, and the succession of Peter and the other Apostles to have expired. But, after this, she will be victoriously exalted in the sight of all doubters."

Comment: According to many prophecies, the Church will be without a Pope for some time, and most of the hierarchy will have been martyred. It will seem that the Church has been destroyed. But she will miraculously rise again and be more powerful than ever.

The perversion alluded to in the opening sentence of the above passage (as I said six years ago in *World Trends*) seems to be the perversion of the mind — an intellectual perversion, that of humanism and secularism which is influencing much of the thinking in the Church of today. I gave evidence of this by quoting the very words of the Council Fathers while the Council was still in session, but I added that the possibility of a moral perversion was hardly to be considered. This was six years ago, however, and the same cannot be said in 1970. Moral perversion now exists within the Church, and this is not surprising since the philosophical concepts of one's intellect are bound to be reflected sooner or later in one's patterns of behaviour. Apart from the many priests who have sought dispensations before getting married, many others in Europe and America have felt that dispensations were not necessary after all. They felt in conscience — so they said — that the dispensation existed in the very circumstances of their lives, and since they were "adult and responsible," it was quite superfluous for them to seek a humiliating formal dispensation from Rome's "autocratic" power. More recently, a news item picked up in a Belgian newspaper reported that one of the "prophets" of the new wave, the author of many theological best-sellers, had been convicted of offensive behaviour for sunbathing nude in the sand dunes of his native country. A fine example for a priest to give!

¶ 34. *Telesphorus of Cozensa* (16th century). "A powerful French Monarch and French Pope will regain the Holy Land after terrible wars in Europe. They will convert the world and bring universal peace. They will overcome the German ruler."

Comment: This is a repeat, or confirmation, of what we have already seen in previous prophecies. The identity of the German ruler, however, is not clear at this stage. One point worthy of note is the absence of references to a general invasion of Western Europe by Soviet Russia. On the other hand, many prophecies lay stress on the chaos and anarchy that will prevail in every country. We can only infer that Communism will triumph *from within*. At the same time, however, a revolution in Russia will shake the foundations of the Communist régime there. Another possibility is that Soviet Russia will be so involved in an Asian conflict that it will be unable to interfere with Western Europe.

¶ 35. *David Poreaus* (17th century). "The Great Monarch will be of French descent, large forehead, large dark eyes, light brown wavy hair and an eagle nose. He will crush the enemies of the Pope and will conquer the East."

Comment: As said before, the great king will be of French descent, but not necessarily French in the narrow sense. Other prophecies mention his having German and Austrian blood as well. One thing seems certain; France will be the cradle of the counter-revolution, as it was the cradle of the revolution in the 18th century.

¶ 36. *Fr. Balthassar Mas* (17th century). "I saw a land swallowed up by the sea and covered with water. But, afterwards, I saw that the sea receded little by little and the land could be seen again. The tops of the towers in the city rose again above the water and appeared more beautiful than before, and I was told that this land was England."

Comment: I think this prophecy must be correlated with that of St. Hildegard, quoted earlier. There exist one or two more mentioning the low-lying lands of England being destroyed by a tidal wave. Many of the capital cities of the world will be destroyed during the coming upheaval, and the destruction seems to have some relationship with the role of each of these cities; thus, London will be destroyed by the sea (England used to rule the seas), Paris by fire (France spread the fire of her false political doctrines throughout the whole world), Rome by an earthquake (the "Rock" of Peter has been split by Paul VI himself).

¶ 37. *St. Margaret Mary* (17th century). "I understand that the devotion of the Sacred Heart is a last effort of His Love towards the Christians of these latter days, by offering to them an object and means so calculated to persuade them to love Him."

Comment: Salvation is in the Sacred Heart, not in some pragmatic "updating," and not in some humanistic rewording of the Holy Mass. Recently, a priest wrote in a Catholic paper: "Our people do not go much to Benediction these days; devotion, generally, is decreasing." And a few lines below, he went on to say: "People are becoming more and more social; they increasingly realize the necessity of living in the modern world . . ." The context of this article made it obvious that the parallel was *not* intentional, but the relation of cause and effect is inescapable: the world seems more important than the Eucharist. This is surely *not* the way to salvation. As a matter of fact, it is quite untrue to say that the Catholic people as a whole are becoming "more social" in the sense understood by this priest. We are all aware, of course, that interdependence is increasing, and that we are living *in* the modern world, but this is no justification for the frantic efforts of the Progressives to make us live *like* the modern world; still less for the unpardonable sacrilege of making the Mass a sort of social gathering. The agitation for a reform of the Mass did not come from the Catholic people; it came from a handful of intellectuals obsessed with Teilhardian concepts. One clear result, however, is the decline in devotional practices in general, and in the devotion of the Sacred Heart in particular.

¶ 38. *Bl. Mary of Agreda* (17th century). "It was revealed to me that through the intercession of the Mother of God all heresies will disappear. The victory over heresies has been reserved by Christ for His Blessed Mother. In the latter days, the Lord will in a special manner spread the renown of His Mother. Mary began salvation, and by her intercession it will be completed. Before the second coming of Christ, Mary, more than ever, must shine in mercy, might, and grace in order to bring unbelievers into the Catholic faith. The power of Mary in the latter days will be very conspicuous. Mary will extend the reign of Christ over the heathens and the Mohammedans, and it will be a time of great joy when Mary is enthroned as Mistress and Queen of Hearts.

"An unusual chastisement of the human race will take place towards the end of the world."

Comment: Many prophecies speak of the special role of Mary in the latter days. Her mercy, power, and grace have indeed been shining with increasing intensity since 1830 in many apparitions: Rue du Bac, La Salette, Lourdes, Pontmain, Knock, Fatima, Banneux, Beauraing, Heede, Marienfried, Garabandal, San Domiano, etc. In spite of this, the Council Fathers deemed it "inopportune" to proclaim Mary as Mediatrix and Co-Redemptrix.

¶ 39. *St. Louis-Marie Grignion De Montfort* (18th century) "The power of Mary over all devils will be particularly outstanding in the last period of time. She will extend the Kingdom of Christ over the idolaters and Moslems, and there will come a glorious era when Mary is the Ruler and Queen of Hearts."

Comment: Here again we have confirmation that the Mohammedans will be converted. This will take place under the reign of the Great King (see previous prophecies), after the invasion of Western Europe and the Arabs' defeat at the hands of the Great Christian King. The following prophecy says the same thing again.

¶ 40. *Capuchin Friar* (18th century).   "All priests, both secular and regular, shall be stripped of their possessions and of every kind of property. They will have to beg from lay people their food and everything necessary for their support and for the worship of God.

"The Pope shall die during these calamities, and the Church will be reduced to the most painful anarchy as a result. Much human blood will be shed in Italy; many cities, towns and castles shall be brought to ruins, causing the death of many thousands of people. By the Catholic clergy and people the true and lawful Pope will be elected who shall be a man of great holiness and goodness of life.

"A scion of the Carolingian race, by all considered extinct, will come to Rome and behold and admire the piety and clemency of this Pontiff, who will crown him, and declare him to be the legitimate Emperor of the Romans. He shall destroy the Ottoman Empire and all heresies. With the assistance of God and of the Pope, he will cooperate in the reformation of abuses; he will assume the direction of temporal governments; he will assign a decent pension to the Pope and also the bishops and clergy. And they all will live in peace which shall last till the End of Time."

Comment: Just one remark here: the death of the Pope will bring about a schism and an anti-pope. The reference to the "true and lawful Pope" in itself justifies this interpretation, but other prophecies are quite explicit about the election of an anti-pope.

¶ 41. *Bernhardt Rembordt* (18th century).   "Cologne will be the site of a terrible battle. Many foreigners will be slaughtered there; both men and women will fight for their Faith. It will be impossible to prevent this horrible devastation. People will wade up to their ankles in blood. At last, a foreign King will appear and win a victory for the cause of the righteous. The remaining enemy will retreat to the Birchtree country. There, the last battle will be fought for the just cause.

"At that time France will be divided. The German Empire will choose a simple man as the Emperor, who will rule for a short time. His successor will be the man for whom the world has longed. He will be called a "Roman Emperor," and he will give peace to the world. A good and happy era will follow. God will be praised on earth, and war will be no more."

Comment: A number of prophecies mention a great battle in the Birchtree country, which is probably in Westphalia. It will be the determining battle between the Christian forces under the Great King and the last armies of the Communist block. This prophecy must be correlated with that of Telesphorus of Cozensa, which referred to a "German Ruler" who will precede the Great King. All these prophecies confirm and complete each other.

¶ 42. *Elizabeth Canori-Mora* (19th century).   "Countless legions of demons shall overrun the earth — the instrument of divine justice — and causing [*sic*] terrible calamities and disasters. Nothing on earth shall be spared. After the frightful punishment I saw a great light appear upon the earth which was the sign of reconciliation of God with men. All men shall become Catholics, and they shall acknowledge the Pope as Vicar of Jesus Christ."

Comment: There exist a few other prophecies announcing the unchaining of demons in the second part of the 20th century. Elizabeth Canori-Mora did not indicate the period, but Anne Catherine Emmerich did. Demons are now roaming the earth, and this accounts for the aberrations to be found even within the Church. The modern world is completely corrupt — intellectually, philosophically and morally. Technology and Democracy were supposed to bring about happiness on earth, but it has brought about such misery that people everywhere are taking to liquor and drugs. Moral corruption is such that its presence is now to be seen — and tolerated — even within the walls of a church; priests now give communion to half-naked girls as a matter of course. The chastisement is inevitable.

In this vein read the following. It was said by Bishop Fulton Sheen long before he took over the See of Rochester, which seems to have brought about a complete change in his thinking, but at that time he often had truly prophetic insights:

"Wild and gloomy times? Small wonder that people are shaken and confused! The signs are everywhere. The signs of our times point to a struggle between absolutes. We may expect the future to be a time of trials and catastrophes for two reasons: firstly, to stop disintegration. . . Revolution, disintegration, chaos must be reminders that our thinking has been wrong, our dreams have been unholy. The second reason why a crisis must come is in order to prevent a false identification of the Church and the World. Our Lord intended that His followers should be different in spirit from those who were not His followers. . . But, though this is the divine intent, it is unfortunately true that the line of demarcation is often blotted out. Mediocrity and compromise characterize the lives of many Christians. . . There is no longer the conflict which is supposed to characterize us. We are influencing the world less than the world is influencing us. Since the amalgamation of the Christian and pagan spirit has set in, since the gold is married with an alloy, the entirety must be thrown into the furnace so that the dross may be burnt away."

¶ 43. *St. Anthony of the Desert* (4th century) [Disquisition CXIV]. "Men will surrender to the spirit of the age. They will say that if they had lived in our day, Faith would be simple and easy. But in their day, they will say, things are complex; the Church must be brought up to date and made meaningful to the day's problems. When the Church and the World are one, then those days are at hand. Because our Divine Master placed a barrier between His things and the things of the world." (Quoted in *Voice of Fatima,* January 23, 1968).

Comment: Most prophecies quoted in this book are translations from other languages, viz., Latin, French, German, Italian, and other languages, as the case may be. Old prophecies like the one quoted above are translated from the Latin. Obviously, the choice of suitable words for rendering the original is a matter for the translator to decide. However, in this case, the words "up to date" and "meaningful" are a little surprising because they are precisely the words used by today's Progressives to justify their reckless innovations. If the rendering is absolutely correct, then St. Anthony was remarkably perspicacious.

¶ 44.1 *The Ecstatic of Tours* (Her name is not known. She

was a nun living in Tours, in France. In the year 1882, using a nom-de-plume, her spiritual director published her revelations in a book called *La Veille de la Victoire du Christ (On the Eve of the Victory of Christ)*. The following excerpts come from the prophecies made in 1872 and 1873.)

¶ 44.2　"Before the war breaks out again, food will be scarce and expensive. There will be little work for the workers, and fathers will hear their children crying for food. There will be earthquakes and signs in the sun. Towards the end darkness will cover the earth.

¶ 44.3　"When everyone believes that peace is assured, when everyone least expects it, the great happenings will begin. Revolution will break out in Italy almost at the same time as in France. For some time, the Church will be without a Pope. England, too, will have much to suffer.

¶ 44.4　"The revolution will spread to every French town. Wholesale slaughter will take place. This revolution will last only a few months but it will be frightful; blood will flow everywhere because the malice of the wicked will reach its highest pitch. Victims will be innumerable. Paris will look like a slaughter-house. Persecutions against the Church will be even greater, but it will not last long. All churches will be closed, but only for a very short time in those towns where disturbances are least. Priests will have to go into hiding. The wicked will try to obliterate everything religious, but they will not have enough time.

¶ 44.5　"Many bishops and priests will be put to death. The Archbishop of Paris will be murdered. Many other priests, in Paris, will have their throats cut because they will not have time to find a hiding place.

¶ 44.6　"The wicked will be the masters for one year and a few months. In those days, France will receive no human assistance. She will be alone and helpless. At this juncture, the French people will turn back to God and implore the Sacred Heart of Jesus and Mary Immaculate. They will at last confess that He alone can restore peace and happiness.

¶ 44.7　"The French people will ask for the good King, he who was chosen by God. He will come, this saviour whom God has spared for France, this King who is not wanted now because he is dear to God's Heart. He will ascend to the throne; he will free the Church and reassert the Pope's rights.

¶ 44.8　"The Council will meet again after the victory. But,

this time, men will be obliged to obey; There will be only one flock and one shepherd. All men will acknowledge the Pope as the Universal Father, the King of all peoples. Thus mankind will be regenerated."

Comment: Australian and American readers may wonder what the relevance of this prophecy is to their parts of the world. Here is my answer: whereas it is not possible to assert that the *same* sequence of events will affect Australia and America, there is no doubt that what is happening in Europe will have far-reaching repercussions throughout the world; European affairs have always done so. Moreover, although most prophecies originate from European countries and describe events in those countries, there are some which make it clear that the *whole* world will be in turmoil, that the revolution will be universal, that persecutions will be waged everywhere on earth, and that a new political order will be set up everywhere.

¶ 45. *St. Francis Of Paola* (Born in Italy, 15th century.) "By the grace of the Almighty, the Great Monarch will annihilate heretics and unbelievers. He will have a great army, and angels will fight at his side. He will be like the sun among the stars. His influence will spread over the whole earth. All in all, there will be on earth twelve Kings, one Emperor, one Pope and a few Princes. They will all lead holy lives."

¶ 46.1 *Venerable Bartholomew Holzhauser* (Born in the 17th century, in Germany). "The fifth period of the Church, which began *circa* 1520, will end with the arrival of the Holy Pope and of the powerful Monarch who is called "Help From God" because he will restore everything [in Christ].

¶ 46.2 "The fifth period is one of affliction, desolation, humiliation, and poverty for the Church. Jesus Christ will purify His people through cruel wars, famines, plague epidemics, and other horrible calamities. He will also afflict and weaken the Latin Church with many heresies. It is a period of defections, calamities and extermination. Those Christians who survive the sword, plague and famines, will be few on earth. Nations will fight against nations, and will be desolated by internecine dissensions.

¶ 46.3 "During this period the Wisdom of God guides the Church in several ways: 1) by chastising the Church so that riches may not corrupt her completely; 2) by interposing the Council of Trent like a light in the darkness, so that the Christians who see the light may know what to believe; 3) by setting St. Ignatius and his Society in opposition to Luther and other heretics; 4) by carrying to remote lands the Faith which has been banned in most of Europe.

¶ 46.4 "Are we not to fear, during this period, that the Mohammedans will come again, working out their sinister schemes against the Latin Church?

¶ 46.5 "During this period, many men will abuse of the freedom of conscience conceded to them. It is of such men that Jude, the Apostle, spoke when he said: 'These men blaspheme whatever they do not understand; and they corrupt whatever they know naturally as irrational animals do. . . They feast together without restraint, feeding themselves, grumbling murmurers, walking according to their lusts; their mouth speaketh proud things, they admire people for the sake of gain; they bring about division, sensual men, having not the spirit.'

¶ 46.6 "During this unhappy period, there will be laxity in divine and human precepts. Discipline will suffer. The Holy Canons will be completely disregarded, and the Clergy will not respect the laws of the Church. Everyone will be carried away and led to believe and to do what he fancies, according to the manner of the flesh.

¶ 46.7 "They will ridicule Christian simplicity; they will call it folly and nonsense, but they will have the highest regard for advanced knowledge, and for the skill by which the axioms of the law, the precepts of morality, the Holy Canons and religious dogmas are clouded by senseless questions and elaborate arguments. As a result, no principle at all, however holy, authentic, ancient, and certain it may be, will remain free of censure, criticism, false interpretations, modification, and delimitation by man.

¶ 46.8 "These are evil times, a century full of dangers and calamities. Heresy is everywhere, and the followers of heresy are in power almost everywhere. Bishops, prelates, and priests say that they are doing their duty, that they are vigilant, and that they live as befits their state in life. In like manner, therefore, they all seek excuses. But God will permit a great evil against His Church: Heretics and tyrants will come suddenly and unexpectedly; they will break into the Church while

bishops, prelates, and priests are asleep. They will enter Italy
and lay Rome waste; they will burn down the churches and
destroy everything.

¶ 46.9   "The sixth period of the Church will begin with the
powerful Monarch and the Holy Pontiff, as mentioned previously, and it will last until the revelation of Antichrist. In this
period, God will console His Holy Church for the affliction
and great tribulation which she has endured during the fifth
period. All nations will become Catholic. Vocations will be
abundant as never before, and all men will seek only the
Kingdom of God and His justice. Men will live in peace, and
this will be granted because people will make their peace with
God. They will live under the protection of the Great Monarch and his successors.

¶ 46.10   "During the fifth period, we saw only calamities and
devastation; oppression of Catholics by tyrants and heretics;
executions of Kings, and conspiracies to set up republics.
But, by the Hand of God Almighty, there occurs so wondrous
a change during the sixth period that no one can humanly
visualize it.

¶ 46.11   "The powerful Monarch, who will be sent by God,
will uproot every republic. He will submit everything to his
authority, and he will show great zeal for the true Church of
Christ. The empire of the Mohammedans will be broken up,
and this Monarch will reign in the East as well as in the West.
All nations will come to worship God in the true Catholic and
Roman faith. There will be many Saints and Doctors (of the
Church) on earth. Peace will reign over the whole earth because God will bind Satan for a number of years until the
days of the Son of Perdition. No one will be able to pervert
the word of God since, during the sixth period, there will be
an ecumenic council which will be the greatest of all coun-
cils. By the grace of God, by the power of the Great Monarch, by the authority of the Holy Pontiff, and by the union
of all the most devout princes, atheism and every heresy will
be banished from the earth. The Council will define the true
sense of Holy Scripture, and this will be believed and accepted
by everyone."

Comment: On many points this prophecy confirms that of
the Ecstatic of Tours. Ven. B. Holzhauser divides Church
history into seven periods. The fifth period, (he is specific

about it), will end with the arrival of the Great Monarch and the Holy Pontiff, both of whom are mentioned in many prophecies. They will work hand-in-hand. The Holy Pontiff will be very firm, and his spiritual directives will be made effective thanks to the temporal power of the Great King, who will be his secular arm, and that is exactly the way it should be: the State should be independent from, but obedient to the Church.

The age of permissiveness will have come to an end. It will be realized that rules and regulations have to be enforced, and not merely left to the discretion of the "free conscience" of man — a perverted notion. That is why the Great King will use force whenever necessary to restore order and discipline. A few remarks are necessary here.

It is true that a system based on force alone has no intrinsic value. The yardstick of its worth is not force, but the principles which inspire the system. When the principles are sound, force is justified.

It is also true, however, that the use of force never succeeds in imposing good principles upon persons hardened in their errors. But it does achieve something: it greatly impedes the destructive efforts of such persons; it protects the people at large from their nefarious influence.

If the West has now reached the point of internal disintegration, it is not because the people at large are, in essence, worse than in former times (human nature does not change); it is because they have been led to believe in errors (such as the belief that one has the right to do as one pleases) by a minority of "intellectuals" who have been allowed to disseminate *freely* their pernicious ideas.

Venerable Holzhauser touches on this point in paragraphs 5, 6, and 7 above. It is those "intellectuals" whom St. Jude castigates: men full of pride, perpetual dissenters, skilful in sophistry, twisting the meaning of words, sowers of discord, blaspheming holy things; these men respect nothing in their studious efforts to appear at all times respectable and objective. What is worse, they hold positions of power and influence, so that even our bishops, the defenders of the faith, dare not upbraid these men too openly when they make a public statement to promote their deadly errors.

After noting that the Council of Trent was a gift of God to enlighten and strengthen the Christians of our times, Ven.

Holzhauser goes on to say that another Council is to take place at the time of the Great Monarch. (The Ecstatic of Tours says the same.) Yet, strangely enough, Vatican I and Vatican II are mentioned nowhere. Why? I submit that there may be a number of reasons. Obviously, Ven. Holzhauser can mention only the most significant events of the fifth period. Now, Vatican I may in no way be compared to Trent. It did define Papal infallibility, but its work was unfinished.

Vatican II purposely refrained from being doctrinal; the accent was on the pastoral side of things. But even in a "pastoral" Council it is impossible to avoid all references to doctrinal matters. Vatican II got out of the difficulty by compromise and ambiguities. The Conciliar Fathers were so divided on so many vital issues that it could not have been otherwise, short of a Papal intervention. (The Pope, however, did intervene in a limited way). Had the Council wanted to be doctrinal, it could not have done so either, unless, again, the Pope had imposed his own decisions. It follows that, doctrinally, Vatican II is insignificant.

Pastorally, it could have achieved a great deal, but the climate of permissiveness, hesitancy, timorousness (which is so typical of our times) is hardly propitious for the imposition of firm guidelines. In other words, Rome has failed to impose the correct implementation of the Council's decrees. What has been imposed constitutes a mockery of what had been decided, and it has been imposed by the sizeable proportion of Ecclesiastics, in the world and in the Vatican itself, who are currently subverting the Church.

The liturgy is a case in point: Vatican II *permitted* an extension of the use of the vernacular, while it *commanded* that Latin should be retained. There is nothing wrong, really, in extending the use of the vernacular to the reading of the Epistle and Gospel. But when this latitude results in the complete elimination of Latin, when it leads to the abandonment of Gregorian Chant (which is inseparable from Latin), and to the adoption of guitar-playing and hand-clapping, it is then clearly in opposition to what Pope John intended when he wrote his encyclical *Veterum Sapientia* on retaining Latin.

The result, of course, is here for everyone to see: confusion in the Church, shocking innovations, defections of priests, a sharp drop in vocations and conversions, etc. The Second Vatican Council, therefore, has indirectly precipitated the crisis which had been brewing for about sixty years. Far from being a "renewal", it marks instead the coming end of the fifth period of the Church, mentioned by Ven. Holzhauser.

It must be understood, however, that it is not my intention to oppose in a sweeping statement *all* the changes which have taken place since Vatican II. Throughout history the Church has had to adopt herself to changing conditions. The changes brought about by St. Pius X, who is now regarded as a Conservative, were unprecedented at the time. Conservatism does not mean immobilism. On the contrary, it implies regular overhauls and renovations. This is so because nothing can be conserved without some work of maintenance and renovation, and the Church is no exception. Obviously, in this changing world of ours some sort of updating was called for. That is why there is no question of rejecting indiscriminately all changes. What is to be deplored, however, is that the wise updating intended by John XXIII has become synonymous with Revolution, and that the necessary changes have become a pretext for a clean break with the past.

Obviously, a Council which asserts nothing doctrinally, at the very time when every doctrine is boldly being challenged, and fails to enforce what it decides pastorally, cannot be a very significant Council in the historical perspective. If we fail to see this just now, it is because we are not yet in the broad historical perspective. We are still in the post-conciliar perspective — far too close for a correct assessment. Ven. B. Holzhauser, however, cast his prophetic eye on the general historical perspective, and this may explain why he did not mention the Second Council of the Vatican.

¶ 47. *Venerable Holzhauser* (Continued). "When everything has been ruined by war, when Catholics are hard-pressed by traitorous co-religionists and heretics, when the Church and her servants are denied their rights, when the monarchies have been overthrown and their rulers murdered, then the hand of Almighty God will work a marvelous change, something seemingly impossible according to human reason. . .

"There will rise a valiant king anointed by God. He will be a Catholic and a descendant of Louis IX, yet a descendant also of an old imperial German family, born in exile. He will rule supreme in temporal matters. The Pope will rule supreme in spiritual matters at the same time. Persecution will cease and justice shall reign. He will root out false doctrines. His dominion will extend from East to West. All nations will adore God their Lord according to Catholic teaching. There will be many wise and just men. People will love justice, and peace will reign over the whole earth, for Divine Power will bind Satan for many years until the coming of the Son of Perdition. . .

"After desolation has reached its peak in England, peace will be restored and England will return to the Catholic faith with greater fervour than ever before. . .

"The Great Monarch will have the special help of God and be unconquerable. . ."

Comment: Venerable Holzhauser correctly saw three hundred years ago that, in our own times, the restoration of Monarchy would seem impossible according to human reason. It does seem impossible. Yet, if we consider the manner in which a handful of doctrinally well-trained and determined Bolsheviks took over Russia in 1917, and if we consider that there exists at present in Europe an equally well-trained and determined association of dedicated Catholics who are sparing no efforts to sow the seeds of renewal and are spreading the sound concepts of Catholic thinkers and philosophers who are just as unknown as Karl Marx was in 1850 — but not less capable, one can see, then, that God has already set the stage for the marvelous renewal which He will work.

¶ 48.1 *Bl. Anna-Maria Taigi* (19th century). "God will send two punishments; one will be in the form of wars, revolutions and other evils; it shall originate on earth. The other will be sent from Heaven. There shall come over the whole earth an intense darkness lasting three days and three nights. Nothing can be seen, and the air will be laden with pestilence which will claim mainly, but not only, the enemies of religion. It will be impossible to use any man-made lighting during this darkness, except blessed candles. He, who out of curiosity, opens his window to look out, or leaves his home, will fall dead on the spot. During these three days, people should remain in their homes, pray the Rosary and beg God for mercy.

¶ 48.2 "All the enemies of the Church, whether known or unknown, will perish over the whole earth during that universal darkness, with the exception of a few whom God will soon convert. The air shall be infected by demons who will appear under all sorts of hideous forms.

¶ 48.3 "Religion shall be persecuted, and priests massacred. Churches shall be closed, but only for a short time. The Holy Father shall be obliged to leave Rome.

¶ 48.4 "France shall fall into a frightful anarchy. The French shall have a desperate civil war in the course of which even old men will take up arms. The political parties, having exhausted their blood and their rage without being able to arrive at any satisfactory settlement, shall agree at the last extremity to have recourse to the Holy See. Then the Pope shall send to France a special legate. . . In consequence of the information received, His Holiness himself shall nominate a most Christian King for the government of France.

¶ 48.5 "After the three days of darkness, St. Peter and St. Paul, having come down from Heaven, will preach in the whole world and designate a new Pope. A great light will flash from their bodies and will settle upon the cardinal who is to become Pope. Christianity, then, will spread throughout the world. He is the Holy Pontiff, chosen by God to withstand the storm. At the end, he will have the gift of miracles, and his name shall be praised over the whole earth.

¶ 48.6 Whole nations will come back to the Church and the face of the earth will be renewed. Russia, England, and China will come into the Church.

Comment: This prophecy does not add anything new to what we already know from the other prophecies quoted in the twelfth issue of *World Trends,* but it does bring further evidence concerning the events to come. One might conceivably entertain doubts if we had only two or three different prophecies, but it would be unreasonable to do so when we possess well over one hundred, coming from different sources.

Among the books written on Anna-Maria Taigi, we have *Wife, Mother and Mystic,* written by Albert Bessières, S.J., and translated into English by Fr. Stephen Rigby. In his introduction, Fr. Rigby quotes an interesting passage from Louis Veuillot's book *The Fragrance of Rome.* This passage is better than anything I could say to acquaint my readers with the extraordinary gifts of Anna-Maria Taigi (I quote):

"Her intellectual gifts were altogether overshadowed by an unexampled miracle. Shortly before she had entered on the way of perfection there began to appear to her a golden globe which became as a sun of matchless light; in this all things were revealed to her. Past and future were to her an open book.

"She knew with certainty the fate of the dead. Her gaze travelled to the ends of the earth and discovered there people on whom she had never set eyes, reading them to the depth of their souls. One glance sufficed; upon whatever she focused her thoughts, it was revealed to her and her understanding. She saw the whole world as we see the front of a building. It was the same with nations as with individuals; she saw the cause of their distresses and the remedies that would heal them.

"By means of this permanent and prodigious miracle, the poor wife of Domenico Taigi became a theologian, a teacher, and a prophet. The miracle lasted forty-seven years. Until her death the humble woman was able to read this mysterious sun as an ever-open book. Until her death she looked into it solely for the glory of God; that is, when charity suggested or obedience demanded it. Should things for which she had not looked, or which she did not understand, appear she refrained from asking explanations.

"The poor, the great of the world, the princes of the Church came to her for advice or help. They found her in the midst of her household cares and often suffering from illness. She refused neither her last crust of bread nor the most precious moment of her time, yet she would accept neither presents nor praise.

"Her most powerful friends could not induce her to allow them to favour her children beyond the conditions in which they were born. When she was at the end of her resources, she told God about it, and God sent what was necessary.

"She thought it good to live from day to day, like the birds. A refugee queen in Rome wished to give her money. 'Madame,' she said, 'how simple you are! I serve God, and He is richer than you.'

"She touched the sick, and they were cured; she warned others of their approaching end, and they died holy deaths. She endured great austerities for the souls of purgatory, and the souls, once set free, came to thank her. . . She suffered in body and soul. . . She realized that her role was to expiate the sins of others, that Jesus was associating her with His Sacritice, and that she was a victim of His company. The pains of Divine Love have an intoxication no words can explain. After Holy Communion there were times when she sank down as though smitten by a prostrating stroke. To tell the truth, her state of ecstasy was continual because her sense of the presence of God was continual. . . All pain was sweet to her. . . She went her way, her feet all bloody; with shining eyes she followed the Royal way.

"Behold, then, the spectacle God raised to men's sight in Rome during that long tempestuous period which began at the time the humble Anna-Maria took to the way of saints!

"Pius VI dies at Valence; Pius VII is a prisoner at Fontainebleau; the revolution will reappear before Gregory XVI reigns. Men are saying that the day of the Popes is over, that Christ's law and Christ Himself are on the wane, that science will soon have relegated this so-called Son of God to the realm of dreams. . . He will work no more miracles.

"But at precisely this time God raised up this woman to cure the sick. . . He gives her knowledge of the past, present and future. She declares that Pius VII will return. She sees even beyond the reign of Pius IX. . . She is God's answer to the challenge of unbelief."

¶ 49.1 *Fr. Nectou, S.J.* (18th century).   (Father Nectou was Provincial of the Jesuits in the south-west of France. The priests who knew him all regarded him as a saint and a prophet. He died in 1777. The following prophecy was made *circa* 1760.)

"When those things come to pass from which the triumph of the Church will arise, then will such confusion reign upon earth that people will think God has permitted them to have their own contrary will, and that the Providence of God is not concerned about the world. The confusion will be so general that men will not be able to think aright, as if God had withheld His Providence from mankind, and that, during the worst crisis, the best that can be done would be to remain where God has placed us, and persevere in fervent prayers. Two parties will be formed in France which will fight unto death. The party of evil will at first be stronger, and the good side will be weaker. At that time there will be such a terrible crisis that people will believe that the end of the world has come. Blood will flow in many large cities. The very elements will be convulsed. It will be like a little General Judgment.

¶ 49.2 "A great multitude of people will lose their lives in those calamitous times, but the wicked will not prevail. They will indeed attempt to destroy the whole Church, but not enough time will be allowed them, because the frightful crisis will be of short duration. When all is considered lost, all will be found safe. This disaster will come to pass shortly after the power of England begins to wane. This will be the sign. As when the figtree begins to sprout and produce leaves, it is a sure sign that summer is near. England in her turn will experience a more frightful revolution than that of France. It will continue long enough for France to recover her strength; then she will help England to restore peace and order.

¶ 49.3 "During this revolution, which will very likely be general and not confined to France, Paris will be destroyed so completely that twenty years afterwards fathers walking over its ruins with their children will be asked by them what kind of a place that was; to whom they will answer: "My child, this was a great city which God has destroyed on account of her crimes."

¶ 49.4 "Yes, Paris will certainly be destroyed; but, before this happens, such signs and portents will be seen, that all good people will be induced to flee away from it. After these most frightful events, order will be restored everywhere. Justice will reign throughout the whole world, and the counter-revolution will be accomplished. The triumph of the Church will then be so complete that nothing like it has ever been seen before. Those Christians who are fortunate enough to survive will thank God for preserving them and giving them the privilege of beholding this glorious triumph of the Church.

¶ 49.5 "A man disliked by France will be placed on the throne; a man of the House of Orléans will be made king. It is only after this event that the counter-revolution will begin."

Comment: This is a very interesting prophecy for many reasons. However, the precision is such as to make one suspect an interpolation made, perhaps 100 years ago, when Legitimists and Orleanists were vying for the French Crown. Fr. Nectou died before the Revolution of 1789, that is, before King Louis XVI had been murdered following a vote in which the Head of the House of Orléans took part. Yet, Fr. Nectou foresaw that the House of Orléans would not be liked in

France. Now, the interesting point is that the House of Orléans became heir to the French Crown when the Count of
Chambord died childless in 1883. Did Fr. Nectou really foresee all this? Does it mean that the heir of the House of Orléans is to redeem the crime of his ancestor? It seems unlikely
to me, but I keep an open mind. Moreover, a prophecy previously quoted says that the Great King will rise from a
Royal Family which is "now considered extinct." This is
surely not the House of Orléans, but it could be a descendant
of Louis XVII who, according to history, died during the
revolution as a child but, on the strength of much evidence,
was in fact smuggled out of his prison, and replaced by a
dying child. Personally, I am inclined to believe that the Great
King will come from neither family, but from another branch
which will be truly European. I find it somewhat difficult to
assume that a French King would be accepted as the Ruler of
the whole of Western Europe. Finally, some prophecies seem
to warrant the inference that an Orléans King will indeed
reign, but only for a very short time, to be superseded by the
Great King. If this is so, then Fr. Nectou's prophecy may be
wholly authentic, for nowhere does he say that the Orléans
King will be the Great King, the Pope's secular arm, the vic-
tor over the Mohammedans, the ruler of Europe, etc.

That all these events are imminent is now beyond question.
Fr. Nectou supplies us with an additional proof: the waning
power of England. England has indeed lost her Empire since
the end of World War Two. What is even worse, she seems
to have lost the sense of her mission. Every Western nation
has a mission, that of bringing civilization to primitive peoples. Whereas a man can not be regarded as inferior on account of skin-color alone, whereas color discrimination is absolutely wrong and unchristian, it is also an indisputable fact
that colored peoples generally are, as a *whole*, more primitive
than white people. Intelligent and unprejudiced Negroes will
not deny it. That is why it is insane to insist on absolute
equality between whites and Negroes when their general
make-up and way of life are so different. For the same reason,
it is insane to insist on majority rule in Africa. The attitude of
the British Government under Wilson shows that England has
lost the sense of her mission. This was evidenced also under
another Labour government, that of Attlee. Naturally, one
cannot expect realism from socialist dreamers. Be that as it

may, I do not think that anyone in his right mind would deny that the loss of the Empire has reduced England to the rank of a second-class power, to economic hardship, and to its concomitant ills. There is every reason to think, for instance, that the legalization of abortion and sterilization has been helped along by England's economic problems. Remedies like these, of course, are worse than the evils they are intended to cure, but a wholly secularized community is unable to perceive this. And so the stage is set for the chastisement which the prophecies say will be very severe for England.

¶ 50. *Sister Marianne* (This holy nun lived in the convent of the Ursulines in Blois. She made many prophecies. Shortly before her death she predicted the fall of Napoleon I and his brief return from the Island of Elba.)

¶ 50.1 "As long as public prayers are said, nothing shall happen. But a time will come when public prayers shall cease. People will say: 'Things will remain as they are.'

"All men will be taken away gradually in small groups. Only old men will remain. Before the great battle the wicked shall be masters (in France). They will do as much harm as they can, but not as much as they would like, because they shall not have enough time. The good Catholics shall be on the point of being annihilated but, O Power of God, a stroke from Heaven will save them. All the wicked shall perish, but also many good Catholics.

¶ 50.2 "Such extraordinary events shall take place that the most incredulous will be forced to say: 'Truly, the finger of God is here.' There shall be a terrible night during which no one will be able to sleep. But these trials shall not last long because no one could endure them. When all shall appear lost, all will be saved.

¶ 50.3 "It is then that the Prince shall reign, whom people did not esteem before, but whom they shall then seek. The triumph of religion will be so great that no one has ever seen the equal. All injustices will be made good; civil laws will be made in harmony with the laws of God and of the Church. Education in the schools will be most Christian, and workers' guilds will flourish again.

Comment: Here again we see the outlines of a new social and political order diametrically opposed to that of our era.

The state will no longer be separated from the Church. Schools will impart a *totally* Christian education (and not merely a few hours of religion separated from the other subjects of the curriculum). Finally, workers' guilds will replace the obnoxious trade unions. There is a capital difference between guilds and unions: guilds *unite* employers and employees in a *vertical* association within *each* industry. Unions pit employees *against* employers in a *horizontal* association grouping *several* industries. Guilds promote order, justice, and social harmony; unions create chaos, injustice, and civil unrest. Here again we have another instance of the failure of our generation 'to think aright.'

¶ 51. *Nursing Nun of Bellay.* This prophecy was written sometime between 1810 and 1830 and was entrusted to Fr. Fulgence, the Chaplain of the Trappist Monastery of Notre-Dame des Gardes, near Angers.

¶ 51.1 "Once again the madmen seem to gain the upper hand! They laugh God to scorn. Now, the churches are closed; the pastors run away; the Holy Sacrifice ceases.

¶ 51.2 "Woe to thee, corrupt city! the wicked try to destroy everything; their books and their doctrines are swamping the world. But the day of justice is come. Here is your King; he comes forward amidst the confusion of those stormy days. Horrible times! The just and the wicked fall; Babylon is reduced to ashes. Woe to thee, city three times accursed!

¶ 51.3 "There was also a great battle, the like of which has never been seen before. Blood was flowing like water after a heavy rain. The wicked were trying to slaughter all the servants of the Religion of Jesus Christ. After they had killed a large number, they raised a cry of victory, but suddenly the just received help from above.

¶ 51.4 "A saint raises his arms to Heaven; he allays the wrath of God. He ascends the throne of Peter. At the same time, the Great Monarch ascends the throne of his ancestors. All is quiet now. Altars are set up again; religion comes to life again. What I see now is so wonderful that I am unable to express it.

¶ 51.5 "All these things shall come to pass once the wicked have succeeded in circulating large numbers of bad books."

¶ 52. *Jeanne le Royer* (Sister of the Nativity). She was born in 1731 and became a nun in 1755. Being illiterate, she dictated her revelations to her spiritual directors. But later, assailed with scruples, she had these early copies thrown into the fire. Some thirty years later, in 1790, her new spiritual director, Fr. Genet, wrote down her revelations again. He had already written four books when his work was cut short by the persecutions waged against the Church by the revolutionaries.

It seems likely that she had predicted the terrible events of the French Revolution in her earlier revelations, which were destroyed. When the fury of the enemies of God was unleashed from 1789 onwards, however, it became clear that she had a mission, and she was probably persuaded to elaborate on her visions. The holy nun died in 1798. Here are excerpts which seem to have a bearing on our own times.

¶ 52.1 "I see that the century which begins in 1800 shall not yet be the last.

The reign of Antichrist is approaching. The thick vapors which I have seen rising from the earth and obscuring the light of the sun are the false maxims of irreligion and licence which are confounding all sound principles and spreading everywhere such darkness as to obscure both faith and reason."

Comment: By 1790, the "false maxims" which she mentions were already being put into practice by the revolutionaries. But these "false maxims" had been formulated long before and were spread freely by a certain school of philosophers in the fashionable drawing-rooms during the reign of Louis XV. These philosophers were invariably Freemasons — a very significant detail which, however, is usually overlooked by modern historians. Yet, if one wishes to understand the development of the Mystery of Iniquity up to our own times, it is essential to know that these destructive ideas, emanating from France and spreading therefrom throughout the world, were essentially Masonic ideas. Since these ideas were Jewish in origin and therefore anti-Christian, it is easy enough to understand why their acceptance in the modern world has led mankind to the brink of abyss. There is, of course, convincing bibliographical evidence of a Judeo-Masonic plot from the 18th century onwards, but it is not readily available. As a result, the mere mention of a "Judeo-Masonic" plot is usually dismissed as right-wing extremism.

Another error, studiously cultivated by the enemies of the

Church, is that the French Revolution was the spontaneous uprising of a down-trodden populace. In actual fact, allowance being made for some well-founded local grievances, the French peasantry were the most prosperous of all the European countries! Far from being a popular uprising, the French Revolution was brought into being by a section of the nobility who, some decades earlier, had lavishly entertained the "philosophers" in their drawing-rooms and imbibed their false ideas! These same noblemen and their ladies, however, lost their heads under the guillotine after themselves having aroused and unleashed the fury of the mobs.

This digression, I think, is necessary for a better understanding of today's turmoil, for the Revolution is still with us. The issues may have changed but the spirit is the same, and it has now permeated the entire world. Behind all this, of course, stands a spiritual power I will make no bones about naming, no matter how old-fashioned it may sound: this is the devil in his eon-old struggle against God. He knows that his time is running short; he is intensifying his efforts and, being intelligent, realizes that his most likely cooperators are to be sought among those who crucified Christ. This he has done throughout the centuries and more particularly since the 18th century, until such time as the Mystery of Iniquity will find its completion in the earthly kingdom of the Jews under Antichrist. Many private prophecies say so, and not a few Doctors of the Church have thought so. Back now to Sister Jeanne.

¶ 52.2 "One day I heard a voice which said: 'The new Constitution will appear to many other than what it really is. They will bless it as a gift from heaven; whereas, it is in fact sent from hell and permitted by God in His just wrath. It will only be by its effects that people will be led to recognize the Dragon who wanted to destroy all and devour all.'

¶ 52.3 "One night I saw a number of ecclesiastics. Their haughtiness and air of severity seemed to demand the respect of all. They forced the faithful to follow them. But God commanded me to oppose them: 'They no longer have the right to speak in my name.' Jesus told me. 'It is against My wish that they carry out a mandate for which they are no longer worthy.'

¶ 52.4 "I saw a great power rise up against the Church. It plundered, devastated, and threw into confusion and disorder the vine of the Lord, having it trampled underfoot by the people and holding it up to ridicule by all nations. Having vilified celibacy and oppressed the priesthood, it had the effrontery to confiscate the Church's property and to arrogate to itself the powers of the Holy Father, whose person and whose laws it held in contempt.

¶ 52.5　"I had a vision: Before the Father and the Son — both seated — a virgin of incomparable beauty, representing the Church, was kneeling. The Holy Ghost spread His shining wings over the virgin and the two other persons. The wounds of Our Lord seemed alive. Leaning on the Cross with one hand, He offered to His Father with the other hand the chalice which the virgin had given to Him. She supported the chalice which the Master held in the middle. The Father placed one hand on the cup and raised the other to bless the virgin.

¶ 52.6　"I noticed that the chalice was only half-filled with blood, and I heard these words spoken by the Saviour at the moment of presentation: 'I shall not be fully satisfied until I am able to fill it right up to the brim.' I understood then that the contents of the chalice represented the blood of the early martyrs, and that this vision had reference to the last persecutions of the Christians, whose blood would fill the chalice, thereby completing the number of martyrs and predestined. For at the end of time, there will be as many martyrs as in the early Church, and even more, for the persecutions will be far more violent. Then the Last Judgment will no longer be delayed.

¶ 52.7　"I see in God that a long time before the rise of Antichrist the world will be afflicted with many bloody wars. Peoples will rise against peoples, and nations will rise against nations, sometimes allied, sometimes enemies, in their fight against the same party. Armies will come into frightful collisions and will fill the earth with murder and carnage.

¶ 52.8　"These internal and foreign wars will cause enormous sacrifices, profanations, scandals, and infinite evils, because of the incursions that will be made into the Church.

¶ 52.9　"As well as that, I see that the earth will be shaken in different places by frightful earthquakes. I see whole mountains cracking and splitting with a terrible din. Only too happy will one be if one can escape with no more than a fright; but no, I see come out of these gaping mountains whirlwinds of smoke, fire, sulphur, and tar, which reduce to cinders entire towns. All this and a thousand other disasters must come before the rise of the Man of Sin (Antichrist)."

Comment: This is what I have called elsewhere the "Great Storm," a period of civil and foreign wars, anarchy and chaos all over the world, and enslavement under Communism, from which God alone can save us. This liberation will come through natural disasters and is to be followed by a period of complete peace and harmony between people and nations under the reign of the Great Monarch and the Holy Pope. At the end of this glorious reign, Antichrist will come. He will be accepted by the Jewish nation as their messiah and king and will control the whole earth.

The above sequence of events is obvious in such a large number of private prophecies, coming from every nation and every past century, that it is impossible for any serious student of private prophecies to have any reasonable doubts that these events will come to pass as revealed. It should be borne in mind in regard to these prophecies, that communications as we know them today were not in existence even fifty years ago. What then of the preceding centuries? Medieval archives unearthed in a small German village in, say, the 16th century could have no relation to records coming from a French or Italian hamlet in a former or later century. But all these prophecies say the same thing. And there are *hundreds* of them!

For my part, I have studied no less than 300 different prophecies. Moreover, the more ancient of these prophecies describe accurately subsequent events such as the Reformation, the French Revolution, the rise of Capitalism and Democracy, and even Communism. The sceptic may say that these prophecies are nonsense, but the nonsense is in his own mind. Or again, he may say that they are only "private", but so are Lourdes and Fatima; so are the Scapular and the Rosary. It matters little, really, whether a revelation is private or public, so long as it has given reasonable evidence of being true. Let us return again to Sr. Jeanne.

¶ 52.10   "I saw in the light of the Lord that the faith and our holy Religion would become weaker in almost every Christian kingdom. God has permitted that they should be chastised by the wicked in order to awaken them from their apathy. And after the justice of God has been satisfied, He will pour out an abundance of graces on His Church, and He will spread the Faith and restore the discipline of the Church in those countries where it had become tepid and lax.

¶ 52.11 "I saw in God that our Mother, Holy Church, will spread in many countries and will produce her fruits in abundance to compensate for the outrages she will have suffered from the impiety and the persecutions of her enemies.

¶ 52.12 "I saw that the poor people, weary of the arduous labours and trials that God sent to them, shall then be thrilled with a joy that God will infuse in their good hearts. The Church will become by her faith and by her love, more fervent and more flourishing than ever. Our good Mother the Church will witness many amazing things, even on the part of her former persecutors, for they will come forward and throw themselves at her feet, acknowledge her, and implore pardon from God and from her for all the crimes and outrages that they had perpetrated against her. She will no longer regard them as her enemies, but she will instead welcome them as her own children.

¶ 52.13 "Now all the true penitents will flow from all sides to the Church, which will receive them into her bosom. The entire community of the faithful will pour out their hearts in hymns of penance and thanksgiving to the glory of the Lord.

¶ 52.14 "I see in God a great power, led by the Holy Ghost, which will restore order through a second upheaval. I see in God a large assembly of pastors who will uphold the rights of the Church and of her Head. They will restore the former disciplines. I see, in particular, two servants of the Lord who will distinguish themselves in this glorious struggle and who, by the grace of the Holy Ghost, will fill with ardent zeal the hearts of this illustrious assembly.

¶ 52.15 "All the false cults will be abolished; all the abuses of the Revolution will be destroyed and the altars of the true God restored. The former practices will be put into force again, and our religion — at least in some respects — will flourish more than ever."

Comment: This "large assembly of pastors" *who will restore the former disciplines and the former practices,* is undoubtedly the Ecumenic Council to which many other prophecies refer:

This Ecumenic Council will also "destroy the abuses of the Revolution," which have been set loose by Vatican II. These abuses cannot be of a political nature, for it is not the function of an ecumenic council to make political decisions. These abuses, therefore, are liturgical. They are the abuses which we are supposed to accept and hail as a "renewal." And they are indeed "of the Revolution," because it is undeniable that the spirit of the Revolution has entered the Church. (In fact the word was recently used by the Holy Father himself.) Moreover, the mention that "former practices will be put into force again" and "false cults abolished" seems to confirm that view. At the same time, it affords hope for the future: the beautiful Latin liturgy, after all, is not so dead as the revolutionaries would like it to be.

¶ 52.16 "I see in God that the Church will enjoy a profound peace over a period which seems to me to be of a fairly long duration. This respite will be the longest of all that will occur between the revolutions from now till the General Judgment. The closer we draw to the General Judgment, the shorter will be the revolutions against the Church. The kind of peace that will follow each revolution will be shorter also. This is so because we are approaching the End of Time, and little time will be left for either the elect to do good or for the wicked to do evil.

¶ 52.17 "One day the Lord said to me: 'A few years before the coming of my enemy, Satan will raise up false prophets who will announce Antichrist as the true Messiah, and they will try to destroy all our Christian beliefs. And I shall make the children and the old people prophesy. The closer we get to the reign of Antichrist, the more will the darkness of Satan spread over the earth, and the more will his satellites increase their efforts to trap the faithful in their nets."

Comment: As I said previously, the evidence drawn from so many prophecies is such that it is truly impossible to deny in good faith — unless through ignorance of these prophecies — that we have now entered the apocalyptic period. The general picture is quite clear — so plain that it requires no interpretation. Some details, however, call for an interpretation; and, in this case, all I can do is offer my personal opinion with no claim to infallibility. Concerning the above passage, it seems to me that false prophets are already with us. They are not announcing Antichrist yet, but they are surely heralding him because many of the new ideas they push forward are quite in keeping with the descriptions of the reign of Antichrist as found in some early Fathers and Doctors. These false prophets will infiltrate the Church more and more, so that the faithful will be hard put to know which of the new trends to reject and which to accept. It is a time of confusion, of sorrow, and of anguish for many. At the same time, however, the Lord will make little children and old people prophesy. Indeed, there have been many reports recently of children and old people prophesying, both in Europe and America. But, here again, we are none the wiser because, short of an authoritative decision from Rome, we have no means of knowing which of these prophecies are genuine and which are not. Indirectly, however, one can still benefit from them because they *all* re-affirm the forgotten traditional truths.

Some prophecies have it to be understood that Antichrist was to be born *circa* 1962. This, admittedly, is highly speculative. Others seem to indicate that the "Great Storm" might take place *circa* 1974 (do not take this as a certainty!). But it is interesting to note that, up to the Ecumenic Council (Vatican II), the Catholic Church was the *only* human organization in which *nothing but the truth* was still taught (the world at large was already wallowing in a quagmire of errors). But, with the supposed birth of Antichrist in 1962, error has now entered even the Church. Likewise, the possible events of 1974 would correspond with Antichrist's puberty — and first public appearance.

I have said that all this is highly speculative, and I would not repeat it but that I am aware that there is an inveterate tendency in all of us to seek knowledge of the future, which leads us to hold as a certainty what is only a possibility. For this reason I feel that another word of caution is not out of place.

¶ 52.18 "When the reign of Antichrist draws near, a false religion will appear which will deny the unity of God and will oppose the Church. Errors will cause ravages as never before.
¶ 52.19 "One day I found myself in a vast plain alone with God. Jesus appeared to me, and from the top of a small hill,

showing to me a beautiful sun on the horizon, He said dole-fully: 'The world is passing away and the time of My second coming draws near. When the sun is about to set, one knows that the day is nearly over and that the night will soon fall. Centuries are like days for me. Look at this sun, see how much it still has to travel, and estimate the time that is left to the world.'

¶ 52.20   "I looked intently and it seemed to me that the sun would set in two hours. Jesus said: 'Do not forget that these are not millenaries, but only centuries, and they are few in number.'

¶ 52.21   "But I understood that Jesus reserved to Himself the knowledge of the exact number, and I did not wish to ask Him more. It sufficed me to know that the peace of the Church and the restoration of discipline were to last a reason-ably long time.

¶ 52.22   "God has manifested to me the malice of Lucifer and the perverse and diabolical intentions of his henchmen against the Holy Church of Jesus Christ. At the command of their master these wicked men have crossed the world like furies to prepare the way and the place for Antichrist, whose reign is approaching. Through the corrupted breath of their proud spirit they have poisoned the minds of men. Like per-sons infected with pestilence, they have communicated the evil to each other, and the contagion has become general. The storm began in France, and France shall be the first theatre of its ravages after having been its cradle. The Church in Coun-cil shall one day strike with anathemas, pull down and destroy the evil principles of that criminal constitution. What a con-solation! What a joy for the truly faithful!"

Comment: The proud spirit which has poisoned the minds of men is undoubtedly Rationalism in its original sense. In-deed, all the other modern errors derive from it. The develop-ment of modern errors is in itself a subject matter that calls for not less than a book. It is impossible to show in a few pages how Rationalism developed into Liberalism and finally led to Marxism. There are natural and supernatural reasons for this. Perhaps, I shall explain all this in another book. When people understand *why* the world is sick, then they may also discover *how* it can be cured. Admittedly, irreligion is the primary cause, but the problem is not so simple as that because many religious people have now accepted the errors of the agnostics even though they may not be agnostics themselves. Never before have men boasted so much of their "maturity" and of their "reasonableness," yet never before have they been so confused and distracted as today.

The revolution which Sister Jeanne is referring to is the French Revolution of 1789, but more generally, it may be regarded as the universal revolution of ideas called "Enlightenment" which is still continuing in our own times. Indeed, the 1789 revolution was nothing but the palpable result of the Enlightenment, but it did help in spreading its errors all over the world. The American revolution, admittedly, was of a different kind, but the foundations of that new-born republic were laid on the principles of the Enlightenment — of Masonic incubation, mingled with a Protestant brand of Christianity which has always been remarkably accommodating with lower denominators. George Washington himself once expressed the fear that the Republic might deteriorate.

¶ 53. *Anna-Katarina Emmerick* (Blessed Sister Emmerick was an Augustinian nun. She was born in Germany in 1774, spent a life of sufferings, and died in 1824 in her native country. She bore the stigmata of Our Lord.

¶ 53.1 *May 13, 1820.* "I saw also the relationship between the two popes. . . I saw how baleful would be the consequences of this false church. I saw it increase in size; heretics of every kind came into the city (of Rome). The local clergy grew lukewarm, and I saw a great darkness. . . Then, the vision seemed to extend on every side. Whole Catholic communities were being oppressed, harassed, confined, and deprived of their freedom. I saw many churches close down, great miseries everywhere, wars and bloodshed. A wild and ignorant mob took to violent action. But it did not last long.

¶ 53.2 "Once more I saw that the Church of Peter was undermined by a plan evolved by the secret sect, while storms were damaging it. But I saw also that help was coming when distress had reached its peak. I saw again the Blessed Virgin ascend on the Church and spread her mantle [over it]. I saw a Pope who was at once gentle, and very firm. . . I saw a great renewal, and the Church rose high in the sky."

Comment: Many prophecies predict an anti-pope and a

schism. Many predict war, bloodshed, and persecutions right in the Vatican. But also many say that "it will not last long" and that "help will come when everything seems hopeless."

¶ 53.3 *Sept. 12, 1820.* "I saw a strange church being built against every rule. . . No angels were supervising the building operations. In that church, nothing came from high above. . . There was only division and chaos. It is probably a church of human creation, following the latest fashion, as well as the new heterodox church of Rome, which seems of the same kind. . .

¶ 53.4 "I saw again the strange big church that was being built there (in Rome). There was nothing holy in it. I saw this just as I saw a movement led by Ecclesiastics to which contributed angels, saints and other Christians. But there (in the strange big church) all the work was being done mechanically (i.e. according to set rules and formulae). Everything was being done according to human reason. . .

¶ 53.5 "I saw all sorts of people, things, doctrines, and opinions. There was something proud, presumptuous, and violent about it, and they seemed to be very successful. I did not see a single Angel nor a single saint helping in the work. But far away in the background, I saw the seat of a cruel people armed with spears, and I saw a laughing figure which said: 'Do build it as solid as you can; we will pull it to the ground.' "

Comment: Two different churches seem to be indicated in this passage. First, a puppet church set up by the Communists, and a "strange church" comprising "all sorts of people and doctrines" (perhaps in the name of Ecumenism), which will follow modern trends. This church is "unholy and humanistic," but it is not Communist inspired, otherwise the Communists would not want to pull it to the ground. This church is either the true Catholic Church after it has been completely subverted from within, or it is a new church claiming to be the true Catholic Church, if two popes are elected at the same time. Some prophecies seem to warrant the inference that the true Catholic Church will disappear completely for a while as an organization, but, although disorganized, it will survive in the persons of the faithful members of the clergy and laity who will go underground.

¶ 53.6 *July 12, 1820.* "I had a vision of the holy Emperor Henry. I saw him at night kneeling alone at the foot of the main altar in a great and beautiful church . . . and I saw the Blessed Virgin coming down all alone. She laid on the Altar a red cloth covered with white linen. She placed a book inlaid with precious stones. She lit the candles and the perpetual lamp. . . Then came the Saviour Himself clad in priestly vestments. He was carrying the chalice and the veil. Two Angels were serving Him and two more were following. . . His chasuble was a full and heavy mantle in which red and white could be seen in transparency, and gleaming with jewels. . . Although there was no altar bell, the cruets were there. The wine was as red as blood, and there was also some water. The Mass was short. The Gospel of St. John was not read at the end. When the Mass had ended, Mary came up to Henry (the Emperor), and she extended her right hand towards him, saying that it was in recognition of his purity. Then, she urged him not to falter. Thereupon I saw an angel, and he touched the sinew of his hip, like Jacob. He (Henry) was in great pain; and from that day on he walked with a limp. . ."

Comment: Henry is the Great Monarch, chosen by God to restore all things in Christ. Other prophecies, too, mention that he will be limping. The Blessed Virgin urges him not to falter because the enemies of the Church are still to be defeated, and his mission is strewn with difficulties. The white and red of the cloths and vestments symbolize the purity of Christ the Priest, and the fire and blood of those times. The red color also symbolizes the age of the Holy Ghost, which is to come after our age of darkness. It is interesting to note, too, that St. John's Gospel "was not read at the end." This new development was foreseen 140 years ago by Sr. Emmerick.

¶ 53.7 *August to October 1820.* "I see more martyrs, not now but in the future. . . I saw the secret sect relentlessly undermining the great Church. Near them I saw a horrible beast coming up from the sea. All over the world, good and devout people, especially the clergy, were harassed, oppressed, and put into prison. I had the feeling that they would become martyrs one day.

¶ 53.8 "When the Church had been for the most part destroyed (by the secret sect), and when only the sanctuary and altar were still standing, I saw the wreckers (of the secret sect) enter the Church with the Beast. There, they met a Woman of noble carriage who seemed to be with child because she walked slowly. At this sight, the enemies were terrorized, and the Beast could not take but another step forward. It projected its neck towards the Woman as if to devour her, but the Woman turned about and bowed down (towards the Altar), her head touching the ground. Thereupon, I saw the Beast taking to flight towards the sea again, and the enemies were fleeing in the greatest of confusion. Then, I saw in the distance great legions approaching. In the foreground I saw a man on a white horse. Prisoners were set free and joined them. All the enemies were pursued. Then, I saw that the Church was being promptly rebuilt, and she was more magnificent than ever before."

Comment: The description of the Beast of the sea and the Woman with Child is strikingly similar to that which is given in the *Apocalypse*. Yet, Sister Emmerick's confidant, whose truthfulness cannot be doubted, said that she had never read it. In this passage the Woman is the Church. She is about to give birth to ("elect") a Pope who will rule with a "rod of iron" (*Apoc.* 12:5), and her travail will coincide with the last persecutions before peace is restored. The legions are those of Henry, the great Catholic prince. Many prophecies say that he will ride a white horse, and this may be taken quite literally, for by that time Europe will be in ruins and there will be nothing else for travelling.

¶ 53.9 *August 10, 1820.* "I see the Holy Father in great anguish. He lives in a palace other than before and he admits only a limited number of friends near him. I fear that the Holy Father will suffer many more trials before he dies. I see that the false church of darkness is making progress, and I see the dreadful influence it has on people. The Holy Father and the Church are verily in so great a distress that one must implore God day and night."

¶ 53.10 "Last night I was taken to Rome where the Holy Father, immersed in his sorrow, is still hiding to elude dangerous demands (made upon him). He is very weak, and exhausted by sorrows, cares, and prayers. He can now trust but few people. That is mainly why he is hiding. But he still has with him an aged priest who has much simplicity and godli-

ness. He is his friend, and because of his simplicity they did
not think it would be worth removing him. But this man receives many graces from God. He sees and notices a great
many things which he faithfully reports to the Holy Father.
It was required of me to inform him, while he was praying,
of the traitors, and evil-doers who were to be found among
the high-ranking servants living close to him, so that he might
be made aware of it."

Comment: When I first published this prophecy in a 1964
edition of *World Trends*, it was not possible to say then that
the Vatican was riddled with traitors. Today, it is much more
credible.

Here is another question likely to be asked: "Is Pope Paul
the Holy Father referred to in this prophecy?" Frankly, I do
not know. In any case, it cannot be taken for granted that he
is.

¶ 53.11 *August 25, 1820.* "I do not know in what manner I
was taken to Rome last night, but I found myself near the
Church of St. Mary Major, and I saw many poor people who
were greatly distressed and worried because the Pope was to
be seen nowhere, and also on account of the restlessness and
the alarming rumors in the city. These people did not seem to
expect the church doors to open; they only wanted to pray
outside. An inner urging had led them there individually. But
I was in the church, and I opened the doors. They came in,
surprised and frightened because the doors had opened. It
seems to me that I was behind the door, and they could not
see me. There was no office on in the Church, but the Sanctuary lamps were lit. The people prayed quite peacefully.

¶ 53.12   "Then, I saw an apparition of the Mother of God,
and she said that the tribulation would be very great. She
added that these people must pray fervently with outstretched
arms, be it only long enough to say three Our Fathers. This
was the way her Son prayed for them on the Cross. They
must rise at twelve at night, and pray in this manner; and
they must keep coming to the Church. They must pray above
all for the Church of Darkness to leave Rome.

¶ 53.13   "She (the Holy Mother) said a great many other
things that it pains me to relate: she said that if only one
priest could offer the bloodless sacrifice as worthily and with

the same dispositions as the Apostles, he could avert all the disasters (that are to come). To my knowledge the people in the church did not see the apparition, but they must have been stirred by something supernatural, because, as soon as the Holy Virgin had said that they must pray God with outstretched arms, they all raised their arms. These were all good and devout people, and they did not know where help and guidance should be sought. There were no traitors and no enemies among them, yet they were afraid of one another. One can judge thereby what the situation was like."

Comment: The first remark to be made here, perhaps, concerns the fact that Sister Emmerick was taken through space and time (i.e. from Germany to Rome, and from her own times to some time in the future). In what manner she was thus carried, she herself did not know. This is reminiscent of St. Paul. But whatever the manner, a person with any knowledge of mystical theology, and believing what a Catholic should, will know that it is possible. The rest of the message alludes once more to the false Church of Darkness which will be set up in Rome, and to the fact that the Pope will no longer be seen in public. Then, we have another reference to the Great Disaster to come, and the confusion of the Faithful who, by then will be left without guidance. Finally, there is the significant reference to the mutual distrust of Christians, significant, because of the well-known Communist "technique" of planting traitors everywhere.

¶ 53.14 *September 10, 1820.* "I saw the Church of St. Peter: it had been destroyed but for the Sanctuary and the main Altar. St. Michael came down into the church, clad in his suit of armor, and he paused, threatening with his sword a number of unworthy pastors who wanted to enter. That part of the Church which had been destroyed was promptly fenced in with light timber so that the Divine office might be celebrated as it should. Then, from all over the world came priests and laymen, and they rebuilt the stone walls, since the wreckers had been unable to move the heavy foundation stones."

Comment: The actual destruction of the Church of St. Peter does not necessarily follow from what is said here, although it remains a possibility. The Church of St. Peter may stand as a symbol of the Catholic Church which — as many privileged souls have warned — will be almost completely destroyed before being reborn more beautiful and more glorious than ever.

¶ 53.15 *September 27, 1820.* "I saw deplorable things: they were gambling, drinking, and talking in church; they were also courting women. All sorts of abominations were perpetrated there. Priests allowed everything and said Mass with much irreverence. I saw that few of them were still godly, and only a few had sound views on things. I also saw Jews standing under the porch of the Church. All these things caused me much distress."

Comment: When I first quoted this, in 1964, things were not half so bad as they are now. True, I already had a photograph showing teenage girls "twisting" in black tights in the sanctuary of a Belgian church, but not, as now, of nuns dancing and throwing up their legs while Mass was being concelebrated by a number of priests in business suits. In 1964 they were not yet consecrating Coca-cola and hot-dog buns. Although it was obvious that many priests had unsound views on many things, their love of freedom had not yet driven any of them to issue ultimata to the hierarchy, or to go on strike, to occupy churches, to canvass protest notes, nor to challenge openly the authority of the Pope and hierarchy. These things are now on record.

¶ 53.16 *October 1, 1820.* "The Church is in great danger. We must pray so that the Pope may not leave Rome; countless evils would result if he did. They are now demanding something from him. The Protestant doctrine and that of the schismatic Greeks are to spread everywhere. I now see that in this place (Rome) the (Catholic) Church is being so cleverly undermined, that there hardly remain a hundred or so priests who have not been deceived. They all work for destruction, even the clergy. A great devastation is now near at hand."

Comment: It is clear that these predictions refer to the same period. However, one may justifiably ask: "Is this *really* our period? Was not the Church in great danger in the 19th century too?" To both questions the answer is yes, for at the time of this prophecy, the arrest of Pius VII was already a thing of the past. As for the events of 1870, it cannot be said that they match the details of the prophecy. On the other hand, the specific mention of Russia (as will be seen later) makes it clear that this is indeed our own period, as it is hardly necessary to point out that Russia was no threat to the Church in the 19th century.

¶ 53.17 *October 4, 1820.* "When I saw the Church of St. Peter in ruins, and the manner in which so many of the clergy were themselves busy at this work of destruction — none of them wishing to do it openly in front of the others — I was in such distress that I cried out to Jesus with all my might, imploring His mercy. Then, I saw before me the Heavenly Spouse, and He spoke to me for a long time. . . He said, among other things, that this translation of the Church from one place to another meant that she would seem to be in complete decline. But she would rise again; even if there remained but one Catholic, the Church would conquer again because she does not rest on human counsels and intelligence. It was also shown to me that there were almost no Christians left in the old acceptation of the word.

¶ 53.18 *October 7, 1820.* "As I was going through Rome with St. Françoise and the other Saint, we saw a great palace engulfed in flames from top to bottom. I was very much afraid that the occupants would be burned to death because no one came forward to put out the fire. As we came nearer, however, the fire abated and we saw the blackened building. We went through a number of magnificent rooms (untouched by the fire), and we finally reached the Pope. He was sitting in the dark and slept in a large arm-chair. He was very ill and weak; he could no longer walk. The ecclesiastics in the inner circle looked insincere and lacking in zeal; I did not like them. I told the Pope of the bishops who are to be appointed soon. I told him also that he must not leave Rome. If he did so, it would be chaos. He thought that the evil was inevitable and that he should leave in order to save many things beside himself. He was very much inclined to leave Rome, and he was insistently urged to do so. The Pope is still attached to the things of this earth in many ways.

¶ 53.19 "The Church is completely isolated and as if completely deserted. It seems that everyone is running away. Everywhere I see great misery, hatred, treason, rancour, confusion, and an utter blindness. O city! O city! What is threatening thee? The storm is coming; do be watchful!

¶ 53.20 *1820-1821 (No precise date).* "I also saw the various regions of the earth. My Guide (Jesus) named Europe, and, pointing to a small and sandy region, He uttered these remarkable words: 'Here is Prussia, the enemy.' Then He showed me another place, to the north, and He said: 'This is Moskva, the land of Moscow, bringing many evils.' "

Comment: Here, the mention of Prussia may lead to the inference that this prophecy applies to the 1870 events. (The Pope lost his temporal power and became a virtual prisoner because the French troops, which were protecting him, were recalled to France during the Franco Prussian war). However, the mention of Russia is unmistakable. Moreover, there exist other prophecies saying that Prussia (or East Germany) will be instrumental in starting World War III.

¶ 53.21 *June 1, 1821.* "Among the strangest things that I saw, were long processions of bishops. Their thoughts and utterances were made known to me through images issuing from their mouths. Their faults towards religion were shown by external deformities. A few had only a body, with a dark cloud of fog instead of a head. Others had only a head, their bodies and hearts were like thick vapors. Some were lame; others were paralytics; others were asleep or staggering.

¶ 53.22 "I saw what I believe to be nearly all the bishops of the world, but only a small number were perfectly sound. I also saw the Holy Father — God-fearing and prayerful. Nothing left to be desired in his appearance, but he was weakened by old age and by much suffering. His head was lolling from side to side, and it dropped onto his chest as if he were falling asleep. He often fainted and seemed to be dying. But when he was praying, he was often comforted by apparitions from Heaven. Then, his head was erect, but as soon as it dropped again onto his chest, I saw a number of people looking quickly right and left, that is, in the direction of the world.

¶ 53.23 "Then, I saw that everything that pertained to Protestantism was gradually gaining the upper hand, and the Catholic religion fell into complete decadence. Most priests were lured by the glittering but false knowledge of young school-teachers, and they all contributed to the work of destruction.

¶ 53.24 "In those days, Faith will fall very low, and it will be preserved in some places only, in a few cottages and in a few families which God has protected from disasters and wars."

Comment: The symbolism of the first paragraph may be interpreted in a number of ways: "Heads like fog" may mean errors of thinking. "Heads only, no bodies and no hearts" may mean high intellect, but divorced from reality and with no charity. "Lame" may mean performance of duty in a half-hearted way. "Paralytics" may mean powerlessness to do anything although the knowledge of what should be done is not impaired. "Asleep" may denote an unawareness of the vital problems which are facing the Church. "Staggering" may mean that the burden of responsibility is too heavy.

The second paragraph may refer to an ecumenic council. Few bishops are sound. The Pope is holy, but old and tired. His head is swaying; he hesitates. He falls asleep; he fails to grasp the really important issues of the day. The others are very much concerned with the world.

Meanwhile, Protestantism is penetrating into the Catholic Church. Like those bishops who have only a head, many priests are more interested in knowledge than in charity, but it is a false knowledge, worldly-wise, overlooking the essentials, similar to the knowledge of young school-teachers who have been taught facts instead of principles, science instead of philosophy.

As a result of all this, Faith will fall very low. But the Faith will survive in a few families which God will protect during the coming disasters.

¶ 53.25 *1820-1821* (No precise date). "I see many excommunicated ecclesiastics who do not seem to be concerned about it, nor even aware of it. Yet, they are (*ipso facto*) excommunicated whenever they cooperate to [*sic*] enterprises, enter into associations, and embrace opinions on which an anathema has been cast. It can be seen thereby that God ratifies the decrees, orders, and interdictions issued by the Head of the Church, and that He keeps them in force even though men show no concern for them, reject them, or laugh them to scorn."

Comment: There is no doubt that this prophecy applies to our times. Writing in past issues of *World Trends,* I have cited many instances of bishops and priests who evinced opinions irreconcilable with Catholic doctrine.

¶ 53.26 *March 22, 1820.* "I saw very clearly the errors, the aberrations, and the countless sins of men. I saw the folly and the wickedness of their actions, against all truth and all reason. Priests were among them, and I gladly endured my suffering so that they may return to a better mind."

Comment: This prophecy only states the presence of errors, without comments. But some other prophecies are more specific; it is not unduly difficult to recognize the errors condemned by Pius XII in *Humani Generis* and by St. Pius X in *Pascendi Dominici Gregis (On Modernism).* I cannot elaborate on this subject; I did so in Issue No. 10 of *World Trends* in which the main errors of our times were examined. In No. 6, I gave evidence that many of the clergy had fallen for these errors. Some young avant-garde priests are now disseminating them freely in parish bulletins in the Diocese of Melbourne.

¶ 53.27 *April 12, 1820.* "I had another vision of the great tribulation. It seems to me that a concession was demanded from the clergy which could not be granted. I saw many older priests, especially one, who wept bitterly. A few younger ones were also weeping. But others, and the lukewarm among them, readily did what was demanded. It was as if people were splitting into two camps."

Comment: This is another significant passage in the light of current developments. Catholics are divided, and this division was brought about by the reckless changes in our liturgy and the doctrinal deviations that were bound to result.

¶ 53.28 *January 27, 1822.* "I saw a new Pope who will be very strict. He will estrange from him the cold and lukewarm bishops. He is not a Roman, but he is Italian. He comes from a place which is not very far from Rome, and I think he comes from a devout family of royal blood. But there must still be for a while much fighting and unrest."

Comment: This is one of the countless prophecies announcing a strong Pope and one of the few adding that he will be of royal blood. But we shall see more of these. This Pope will make use of his God-given power, the mandate every Pope receives from Christ and which he has the duty to use unhesitatingly and resolutely.

¶ 53.29 *October 22, 1822.* "Very bad times will come when non-Catholics will lead many people astray. A great confusion will result. I saw the battle also. The enemies were far more numerous, but the small army of the faithful cut down whole rows (of enemy soldiers). During the battle, the Blessed Virgin stood on a hill, wearing a suit of armor. It was a terrible war. At the end, only a few fighters for the just cause survived, but the victory was theirs."

Comment: This is probably the decisive "Birch-Tree Battle," which is described in countless prophecies. It will be fought in Westphalia (Germany) under the royal leader who is to become Emperor of the West. All the odds will seem to be against him, but after taking his troops to Mass, he will nevertheless engage the enemy and win. German and Russian troops will flee in disarray. Both the Birch-Tree Battle and the rule of the Great Monarch have been described by so many prophecies from the sixth century onward that it is quite unreasonable to dismiss these predictions as nonsense. Only ignorance can be an excuse. The fact is, contrary to a widely held notion, Communism is *not* "here to stay," and Democracy is going through its last senile stage. Both the West and the East are diseased, adhering obstinately to their respective follies, or seeking co-existence between their two dying systems, and unable to see that something else is coming.

¶ 53.30 *April 22, 1823.* "I saw that many pastors allowed themselves to be taken up with ideas that were dangerous to the Church. They were building a great, strange, and extravagant Church. Everyone was to be admitted in it in order to be united and have equal rights: Evangelicals, Catholics, sects of every description. Such was to be the new Church. . . But God had other designs."

Comment: This passage is so plain that no elaboration seems necessary. Sister Emmerick alluded earlier to the same error. All efforts currently made in a spirit of appeasement to unite the churches will be cut short by the Great Holocaust. Reunion will never come about through compromise.

Conclusion: We have reached the end of our encounter with Anna-Katharina Emmerick. What she has told us is anything but heartening. However, there is no cause for despair for the Catholic who is strong in Faith. The *cross* is our symbol. It is an instrument of torture, but it is also the instrument of salvation. Catholics must never forget this trilogy: *"Sacrifice, suffering, salvation."*

¶ 54. *Fr. Freinademetz* (20th century).   "All foreign missionaries shall soon be expelled from China. You will have to walk hundreds of miles before you can find a priest. Even then, your journey will often be fruitless. Some priests and some Catholics shall apostatize. A war shall break out once all foreign missionaries have been expelled. Then, some foreign powers shall occupy the whole of China and shall divide it into zones. One of the occupying powers will be pitiless, and very hard on the people. But during this period, nearly the whole of China shall turn to Christianity."

Comment: This prophecy was made in 1906 in China where Fr. Freinademetz was a missionary. It is certainly significant today. In my opinion, Russia will be the "pitiless" occupying power, but it is not possible to say whether Russia will be converted first, then join the allies to crush Chinese Communism, or will wage war first and be converted later. I am inclined to think that it will be as follows: Soviet Russia fights Communist China. At the same time, or shortly afterwards, the period of chaos and anarchy begins in Western Europe. Soviet Russia meets with great difficulties in China, and the war goes on and on. Revolution breaks out in Russia. Communism collapses. The new Russian government asks for the assistance of the U.S.A. and other powers — which is granted. All together, they defeat China and occupy the land. But the occupying Russian troops have not yet renounced their former ways of dealing with their enemies, hence their ruthlessness.

¶ 55. *The Prophecy of Premol* (5th century).   "Everywhere there is war! Peoples and nations are pitted against each other. War, war, war! Civil and foreign wars! Mourning and death everywhere! Famine over the whole world. Will Lutetius (Paris) be destroyed? Why, O Lord, dost Thou not stop all this with Thy arm? Must also the elements be the instrument of Thy wrath? Enough, O Lord, enough! The cities are destroyed, the natural elements are set loose, the earth quakes everywhere. But mercy, mercy for Rome! But Thou hearest not my entreaties, and Rome also collapses in tumult. And I see the King of Rome with his Cross and his tiara, shaking the dust off his shoes, and hastening in his flight to other shores. Thy Church, O Lord, is torn apart by her own children. One camp is faithful to the fleeing Pontiff, the other is subject to the new government of Rome which has broken the Tiara. But Almighty God will, in His mercy, put an end to this confusion and a new age will begin. Then, said the Spirit, this is the beginning of the End of Time."

Comment: From this prophecy, it is clear that the true Church will be faithful to the Pope in exile; whereas, the new Pope in Rome will be, in fact, an anti-pope. But, since a number of other prophecies tell us that the true Pope will die in his exile, it follows then that the true Church will be leaderless for some time. Then, it is not difficult to anticipate what the anti-pope and renegade hierarchy and clergy will say: "See, your so-called Pope is dead; and who can give you a new Pope now? Our cardinals have already elected the new Pope, he is here in Rome." And, indeed, since the true Church will be completely disorganized, and the faithful Cardinals isolated, no new true Pope could be elected, and thus a large number of Catholics will be misled into accepting the leadership of the anti-pope. Such a schism could not happen if the Pope followed A. C. Emmerick's advice "to stay in Rome". "But", she said, "the Pope is still attached to the things of the earth." And, as is said elsewhere, "He will want to save what he thinks can be saved." In other words, the true Pope, whoever he is at that time, will use his human judgment and leave Rome, instead of remaining firm in the face of the invaders.

¶ 56. *Maria Steiner* (19th century). "I see the Lord as He will be scourging the world and chastising it in a fearful manner so that few men and women will remain. The monks will have to leave their monasteries, and the nuns will be driven from their convents, especially in Italy. The holy Church will be persecuted, and Rome will be without a shepherd. But the Lord showed me how beautiful the world will be after this awful punishment."

¶ 57. *Werdin D'Otrante* (13th century). "The Great Monarch and the great Pope will precede Antichrist. The nations will be at war for four years and a great part of the world will be destroyed. The Pope will go over the sea carrying the sign of Redemption on his forehead. The Great Monarch will come to restore peace and the Pope will share in the victory. Peace will reign on earth."

¶ 58. *Blessed Johannes Amadeus de Sylva* (15th century). "In the Latter Days there shall be great wars and bloodshed. Whole provinces shall be left despoiled and uninhabited, and cities deserted by the people. The nobility shall be slaughtered and influential people ruined, with many changes of kings, commonwealths and rulers.

"Germany and Spain will unite under a great prince chosen by God. But, because of Germany's unfaithfulness, the war will be prolonged until all countries unite under the Great Ruler. After this union, mass conversions will take place by the command of God, and peace and prosperity will follow."

¶ 59. *Sister Rosa Asdenti Di Taggia* (19th century). "A great revolution shall spread over all of Europe, and peace will not be restored until the white flower, the Lily, has taken possession of the throne of France. Not only religious communities but also good lay Catholics shall have their properties confiscated. A lawless democratic spirit of disorder shall reign supreme, and there will be a general overthrow.

"There shall be great confusion of people against people, and nations against nations, with clashing of arms and beating of drums. The Russians and Prussians shall come to Italy. Some bishops shall fall from the Faith, but many more will remain steadfast and suffer much for the Church. Priests and religious shall be butchered, and the earth, especially in Italy, shall be soaked with their blood."

Comment: Here again we have confirmation of East Germany's work of destruction (called Prussia as in all the other prophecies). It is interesting to note that the majority of Bishops will remain steadfast. Perhaps when the chips are down, they will perform better than they did during the Vatican II Council.

¶ 60. *Sister Marianne Gaultier* (18th century). "So long as public prayers are said, nothing shall happen. But a time will come when public prayers shall cease. People will say: 'Things will remain as they are.' It is then that the great calamity shall occur. Before the great battle, the wicked shall be the masters, and they will do all the evil in their power, but not so much as they will desire because they shall not have enough time. The good and faithful Catholics, less in number, shall be on the point of being annihilated, but a stroke from Heaven will save them. Such extraordinary events shall take place that the most incredulous shall be forced to say: 'The finger of God is there.' O power of God! There shall be a terrible night during which no one shall be able to sleep. These trials shall not last long because no one could endure them. When all shall appear lost, all will be saved. It is then that dispatches shall arrive, announcing good news. It is then that the Prince shall reign, whom people will seek that before did not esteem him. The triumph of religion shall be so great that no one has ever seen the equal. All injustices shall be righted; civil laws shall be enacted in harmony with the law of God and of the Church. The education given to children will be most Christian. Pious guilds for workmen shall be restored."

Comment: Many of the prophecies which I have so far quoted are repetitive, but every one of them adds something new besides the description of the main events. Here we have an interesting reference to public prayers; they will cease because people will think that things will remain as they are anyway. Seen in the light of the current crisis in the Church, this statement is significant. How many times have we not heard it said: "Communism is here to stay; we must seek a compromise; we must reach some understanding; we must 'dialogue' and work together for the betterment of mankind." I could cite actual quotations of such instances of wishful thinking. Not a few priests have been led to believe that Communism indeed works for the betterment of mankind! Not a few priests are of the opinion that individual prayer is futile, and social action the only possible answer to the world's ills. Even Rome has decided that it is no longer necessary to pray for the conversion of Russia after each Mass. Rome has even received Soviet dignitaries with smiles and gifts while their henchmen were torturing priests in Bulgaria and elsewhere. The very day that a priest was challenged to renounce his faith or die (I think it was in Bulgaria), Pope Paul VI was shaking hands with Podgorny in the Vatican. This heroic priest's answer was: "I believe in God, I believe in the Holy Catholic Church. My master is the Pope and the Pope will never shake hands with murderers. Why should *I*?" He was slaughtered on the spot. Meantime, Paul VI was exchanging diplomatic smiles with the murderers.

¶ 61. *Brother Louis Rocco* (19th century). "Terrible wars will rage all over Europe. God has long been patient with the corruption of morals; half of mankind He will destroy. Russia will witness many outrages. Great cities and small towns alike will be destroyed in a bloody revolution that will cause the death of half the population. In Istanbul (Constantinople) the Cross will replace the half-moon of Islamism, and Jerusalem will be the seat of a King. The southern Slavs will form a great Catholic Empire and drive out of Europe the Turks (Mohammedans), who will withdraw to North Africa and subsequently embrace the Catholic faith."

¶ 62. *Marie de la Faudais* (19th century). "There will come three days of compelte darkness. Only blessed candles made of wax will give some light during this horrible darkness. One candle will last for three days, but they will not give light in the houses of the Godless. Lightning will penetrate your houses, but it will not put out the blessed candles. Neither wind, nor storm, nor earthquake will put out the blessed candles. Red clouds, like blood, will cross the sky, and the crash of thunder will shake the earth to its very core. The ocean will cast its foaming waves over the land, and the earth will be turned into a huge graveyard. The bodies of the wicked and of the righteous will cover the face of the earth. The famine that follows will be severe. All plant-life will be destroyed as well as three-fourths of the human race. This crisis will be sudden and the punishment will be world-wide."

¶ 63. *Ossolinski Prophecy* (19th century). "The Western Lion, betrayed by its emancipated slaves, shall unite with the Cock and put a young man on the throne. This time, the strength of the disturbers of the earth is broken forever. Brother shall shake hands with brother, and the enemy shall withdraw to a far-away country. At the Rising Sun the Hammer is broken. When the Black Eagle and the Hammer invade foreign countries, they shall perish on a river. The Bear falls after its second expedition. The Danube shines again in splendor. The Barbarians, stricken with great fear, flee in disarray to Asia."

Comment: The symbolism of this prophecy presents no difficulties, but not everyone is acquainted with the language of many prophets. Here, therefore, is the translation.

England, ("the Western Lion") betrayed by her former colonies (which are still formally members of the Commonwealth), will unite with France and put a young Prince on the Throne. The strength of the Communists is broken forever, and the enemy withdraws to a distant country. In China, the Communist "Hammer" is broken. When Communism unites with Prussia (East Germany), they will both be defeated on the banks of the Rhine River (a correlation from other prophecies). Soviet Russia will collapse after her second expedition. The Chinese, stricken with fear, flee back to their country.

From this, and from inferences drawn from other prophecies, it seems that Soviet Russia and Communist China will be at war, and Russia will suffer military set-backs. At the same time, or shortly before, East Germany will wage war in the West with the support of Soviet Russia, but they will both be defeated in Westphalia by the Great King who will be in command of all the Western forces. These events will take place towards the end of the Great Disaster, not at the beginning. There will be a bloody revolution in Russia, perhaps as a result of her military defeats. Communism will be overthrown. The new government will ask for U.S. support against China, and the Chinese will be defeated, their country occupied.

¶ 64. *Maria de Tilly* (19th century). "I see a great darkness and lightning. Paris will be almost entirely destroyed by fire. Marseilles also will be destroyed, and other cities as well."

Comment: The darkness is that of the prolonged night when tremendous lightning will streak across the sky from east to west and north to south.

¶ 65. *Countess Francesca de Billiante* (20th century). "I see yellow warriors and red warriors marching against Europe. Europe will be completely covered with a yellow fog that will kill the cattle in the fields. Those nations which have rebelled aginst the law of Christ will perish by fire. Europe will then be too large for them who survive. May the Lord grant to my grand-children the grace of persevering in the true Faith."

¶ 66. *American Prophecy* (20th century). "The yellow hordes of the Rising Sun and the troops of the middle kingdom will pour out their wrath on the people of the island kingdom which had gathered riches through trade."

Comment: I have mislaid the exact references concerning this prophecy which I received many years ago. But I am quoting it because it confirms others of the same kind.

¶ 67. *Helen Wallraff* (19th century). "Some day a pope will flee from Rome in the company of only four cardinals . . . and they will come to Koeln [Cologne]."

Comment: This prophecy lends credibility to what I have said before: only four cardinals will be with the Pope. The other faithful cardinals will be isolated in various countries, and unable to communicate because of the chaotic conditions prevailing then, and they will be in no position to elect a new Pope when the Pope of that time dies in his exile. As a result, the Roman anti-pope will be able to persuade many Catholics that he is the true Pope. This prophecy says that the Pope will come to Cologne (Koeln in German). There are others, too, which say that he will go to Germany; but many more insist that he will go overseas. Perhaps, he will go to Germany *before* going overseas.

¶ 68. *Bishop George M. Wittman* (19th century). "Very sad times are coming for the Holy Church of Jesus Christ. The Passion of Our Lord will be renewed in a most painful manner in the Church and in her supreme Head. Brutal hands will be laid upon his person. Secret societies will work great ruin, and they will exercise a great financial power."

Comment: It is not possible here to discuss the very important question of economics. Economics, admittedly, is a complex science, and the various existing schools teach conflicting principles. One thing is certain; today's economics are not designed for the furtherance of popular prosperity, but for the benefit of a few manipulators. The working force provides the real wealth of a nation. The working force provides the goods and should be able, therefore, to enjoy the benefits which these goods bring with them. In actual fact, most salaries are totally inadequate, with the result that more goods are produced than can be sold. Alternatively, goods are produced which do not contribute at all to popular prosperity, but only help the manipulators to increase their strangle-hold on the working force. Banks, for instance, which are necessary to a point and deserve a decent remuneration for the services they provide, are accumulating wealth all out of proportion to the work they do. They are continually putting up new skyscrapers for more office suites, more businesses, and more exploitation of the working class, while the man in the street cannot even afford a house for his family. We hear a great deal about "development" and "national prosperity," but such development and prosperity benefit only the financiers. In fact, the so-called "national prosperity" is in the hands of a very few, and it is no right-wing extremism to claim that money is controlled by a Judeo-Masonic clique.

¶ 69. *Franciscan Friar* (18th century). "All the religious orders will be suppressed, except one, the rule of which will be as rigid and severe as that of the monks of the past. During these calamities the Pope will die. As a result, the most painful anarchy will prevail within the Church. Three Popes will vie for the pontifical throne, one German, one Italian, and another Greek. They will all be installed by the armed might of three factions."

¶ 70. *Ida Peerdeman* (20th century). "I clearly see the land of Italy before my eyes. It is as if a terrible storm were breaking out. I am forced to listen, and I hear a word: 'Exile.' "

¶ 71. *Blessed Gaspar Del Bufalo* (19th century). "The death of the impenitent persecutors of the Church will take place during the three days of darkness. He who outlives the darkness and the fear of these three days will think that he is alone on earth because the whole world will be covered with carcasses."

Comment: This prophecy confirms what I have said before: the passage of the comet will be the turning point, God's answer to the arrogance of the wicked, the end of the persecutions and wholesale murders. But why does Blessed Gaspar use the word "carcasses" instead of "bodies?" Because, as I believe, human bodies will be in many cases indistinguishable from animal carcasses — being burnt and blackened by the fires that will rage over the land.

¶ 72. *Sister Marie of Jesus Crucified* (19th century). "All the nations will be shaken by war and revolution. During the three days of darkness, the followers of the evil cause will be annihilated, so that only one-fourth of mankind will survive."

¶ 73. *Brother Anthony of Aachen* (19th century). "Some day war will break out again in Alsace. I saw the French in Alsace with Strassburg at their rear, and I saw Italians fighting with them. Suddenly, great transports of troops arrived from the French side. A two-day battle ended with the defeat of the Prussian army. The French pursued the Prussians over the Rhine in many directions. In a second battle, at Frankfurt, the Prussians lost again and retreated as far as Siegburg, where they joined with a Russian army. The Russians made common cause with the Prussians. It seemed to me as if Austrians also were helping the French. The battle of Siegburg was more terrible than any before, and its like will never occur again. After some days, the Prussians and Russians retreated and crossed to the left bank of the Rhine below Bonn. Steadily pressed by their opponents, they retired to Cologne, which had been bombed so much that only one-fourth of the city remained intact. Constantly in retreat, what was left of the Prussians moved to Westphalia where the last battle went against them. People greatly rejoiced because they were freed from the Prussians. Then, a new Emperor, about forty years old, was elected in Germany, and he met the Pope. Meanwhile, epidemics broke out in the regions devastated by war and many people died. After the battle of Westphalia, the French returned to their country, and from then on there was peace between the French and the Germans. All exiles returned to their homes. When I begged God to take the terrible vision away, I heard a voice saying: 'Prussia must be humiliated in such a manner that it will never again bring sorrow to the Church.'

"In the following year, the Russians will war with the Turks, driving the latter out of Europe and taking Constantinople. The new German Emperor will mobilize for war, but the Germans will not go beyond their frontiers. When afterwards I was shown France and Germany, I shuddered at the losses that had taken place. Soon after the Russian-Turkish war, England also will be visited by war."

Comment: A question arises: who are the soldiers called "the Prussians?" Are these East Germans only? It is fairly certain that East Germany will move first, but it must not be forgotten that Prussia does not consist of East Prussia only; it comprises also Brandenburg, Pomerania, Grenzmark, Silesia, Saxony, Schleswig-Holstein, Hanover, Westphalia, Hesse-Nassau, Rhineland and Hohenzollern; in fact the whole of Northern Germany. Many of these states are now part of West Germany. Will West Germany, then, remain faithful to the West? It is difficult to say. The fortunes of politics can change almost overnight in a democracy. Under Chancellor Adenauer West Germany was quite decidedly pro-Western, but will she remain so under another leader? This is doubtful; there is much in these prophecies which appears to indicate that West Germany will sign an agreement with, and subsequently be dominated by, East Germany. In the context of these prophecies, therefore, the word "Prussia" should not be interpreted in the restrictive sense of "East Germany," but rather in the broader sense of "Germany," especially northern Germany, with the possible — but possible only — exception of Bavaria and other southern Catholic states.

¶ 74. *Fatima* (20th century). Our Lady said: "If my requests are granted, Russia will be converted and there will be peace. If not, Russia will spread her errors in every country, raising up wars and persecution against the Church; many will be martyred. The Holy Father will have much to suffer, and many nations will be destroyed."

Comment: This message was given shortly *before* Communism took over in Russia. The revelations of Fatima have been confirmed by Pius XII, John XXIII, and Paul VI. No Catholic worthy of the name can ignore them. This does not mean, however, that the other revelations given in this book are open to doubt. Quite the opposite; most of them have been taken from Catholic hagiography and are completely reliable too. But Fatima is more recent and has been given a wider publicity. Although less explicit than many others, the words have been sanctioned by a spectacular miracle, the reality of which can be ascertained from the Portuguese newspapers of that time, which were by no means favorably disposed to the Church. The message of Fatima in its entirety can be summed up as follows:

- Do penance and pray the Rosary. Or else . . .
- Russia will spread her errors throughout the world.
- Terrible persecutions will take place.
- Many nations will be destroyed.
- The Pope will have much to suffer.
- The Church will be split into two camps.
- But peace will finally be given to the world.

Many other messages have been given to the world since 1917: Beauraing, Banneux, Osnabrück, Girkalnis, Bonate, Caderosa, Heede, Pfaffenhofen, Montichiari, Espis, Gimigliano, Sisov, Sicily, Necedah, Garabandal, San Damiano, Mexico, Quebec, New Norcia, and many others. Some have been already approved by the Church, some are still being investigated, others have been the object of a negative judgment, and still others have been condemned.

All these recent messages, however, *confirm* what the other prophecies say.

2

THE COMET

Comets are fiery bodies hurtling through space which, unlike the stars, are of low density, and, unlike the planets, have orbits around the sun that are very eccentric. Comets consist of three different parts: the head, the "hair" and the tail. The hair is formed of gases the brightness of which lessens the farther it reaches from the head.

When passing close to the sun, a comet emits a tail which always remains in the direction of the sun, and not necessarily *behind* the comet. The tail does not later return to the comet, but disperses into space. When the tail of a comet crosses the path of a planet, its remnants crash to the ground.

More than sixty comets are known to belong to our solar system, and they re-appear at intervals up to eighty years. But it is estimated that there exist hundreds of thousands of comets, and it is not known whether some will ever re-appear. About 500 are sighted through telescopes every 100 years, and it is thought that their average cycle is equal to tens of thousands of years.

It can be assumed that the larger of these comets would cause such disturbances in the solar system that life on the planets would be greatly affected. However, many civilizations would have time to develop, flourish and perish between two consecutive passages of such long-cycle comets, and the passage of a comet need not mean the *complete* annihilation of human life. Indeed, almost all the ancient civilizations known to man have left evidence of such destruction by comets. It is quite likely that the destructions recorded in the Book of *Exodus* were caused by a comet.

Comets cause fears which are often quite groundless, but it must not be inferred that such fears are always due to ignorance or superstition. The Comet of Brook, for example, hit Jupiter in 1886 and, as a consequence, the Comet's cycle was changed from twenty-nine to seven years; whereas Jupiter was delayed by only two minutes (which shows the disproportion between the mass of a comet and that of a planet).

Nevertheless, such an encounter is more than sufficient to wipe out all traces of life on a planet. If the comet's atmosphere is composed of methane, as is sometimes the case, the earth's atmosphere would be irremediably poisoned.

Concerning *Exodus*, let us recall briefly a situation which afflicted the Egyptians, the crossing dry-shod of the Red Sea and the prolonged duration of the day. In Mexico, on the other hand, a prolonged night was recorded, as evidenced by archeological discoveries. The passage of a comet at that time was recorded, not only in the book of *Exodus*, but also in other documents: an Egyptian papyrus, a Mexican manuscript, a Finnish narration, and many others. The book of *Exodus*, it is true, does not speak of the comet itself, but only of what certainly appears to be its logical effects. We have seen that Nostradamus and other prophets use the term "bloody" and "ferruginous" when speaking of the light of the comet which is to come, but it is never referred to as "fiery red." This is in perfect accord with ancient records on the *Exodus* comet: *"Non igneo sed sanguineo rubore fuisse."* ("It was not the redness of fire, but the redness of blood.")

Will the comet to come be the same as that of *Exodus?* It is not impossible, when we consider the description of the plagues as given in *Exodus* and those described in our Christian prophecies. When the tail of the *Exodus* comet crossed the path of the earth, a red dust, impalpable, like fine flour, began to fall. It was too fine to be seen, which is why it is not named in *Exodus* (7:21), but it colored everything red, and the water of the Egyptians was changed into "blood." The fish died and the water was poisoned by the decomposition of their flesh. It is for this reason that the Egyptians had to "scratch the earth," that is to say, to open new wells. A similar occurrence was recorded in various parts of the world. After the fine rusty pigment fell over Egypt, there followed a coarser dust — "like ash," this is recorded in *Exodus*, for then it was visible. This ash irritated the skin and eyes of both men and animals. They scratched themselves and sores formed; boils appeared and changed into pustules for want of being treated. Soon, the infection spread to the whole body and death followed. After that ash-like substance came a shower of fine sand, then coarse sand, grit, gravel, small stones, large stones, and finally, boulders. The narrative of the Book of *Exodus* confirms this and is in turn corroborated by various documents found in Mexico, Finland, Siberia, Egypt, and India. It is therefore certain that a comet crossed the path of the earth more than 3,000 years ago, causing widespread destruction. This is the kind of phenomenon (if the prophecies are accurate) which is soon to strike the earth again. And now, as it was then, this exceptional occurrence will be permitted by God as a punishment for the sins of men.

Mountains will literally split open; the sea will overrun whole provinces and possibly even small nations such as Holland; some coastal plains will just collapse into the sea; the sky will be on fire in many places when the oxygen of the earth's atmosphere will ignite the hydrogen of the comet's tail. As a result, tremendous hurricanes will be induced, adding to the devastation. The oxygen supply being used up in those regions where the sky fire will rage, people who leave their houses will die from asphyxiation, which is probably why many prophecies say: "Stay indoors; keep your windows shut." But the hurricanes will promptly bring back fresh supplies of oxygen with the effect that this ordeal will be of very short duration. Then, torrential rains will fall, quenching the many fires on earth, but, at the same time, causing widespread flooding. After all these disasters, food will be so scarce that a general famine will follow. Millions of people will starve to death; their unburied bodies will cause pestilence and epidemics all over the land. And so, the loss of life through natural disturbancs will be such as to make appear negligible the number of lives lost through human acts of war. For the above reasons, it would have been misleading to call the Great Disaster "World War III."

Admittedly, the prophecies do not give a description of the many plagues that will strike mankind in the manner I have just detailed, and I may possibly be wrong in some details; but the prophecies do insist on the occurrence of those plagues, namely, fire in the sky, fires on earth, hail of stones, violent lightning, complete darkness, gigantic earthquakes, tidal waves, droughts, floods, air made irrespirable, tremendous hurricanes, famines, epidemics, and the presence of a comet. In other words, the prophecies *list* the various plagues but without giving an overall picture. In my opinion, the comet will be responsible for the other plagues in the order which I have tentatively indicated. Let me elaborate on this point in tabloid form for greater clarity:

- *The Comet approaches the earth:* Climatic changes take place. Droughts and floods occur. Summer is cold because the comet's gases interfere with normal solar radiation.
- *The Comet is now very close:* Climatic changes worsen. Food shortage begins. Winter is hot because the comet is now close enough to radiate its own heat.
- *Hail of stones:* This occurs either before or after the sky fire, and is preceded by a rain of dust, and caused by the comet's tail.
- *Sky fire:* The hydrogen of the comet's tail mixes with the oxygen of the earth's atmosphere and is ignited.
- *Violent lightning:* Caused by electrical discharges between the earth and the comet's head.
- *Air made irrespirable:* Caused by a shortage of oxygen in the earth's atmosphere or by deadly gases, such as methane.
- *Fires on earth:* The land has been heated by the comet's head and is very dry and hot. Lightning strikes. Fields, forests, and cities flare up.
- *Droughts:* Same reason as above, plus climatic changes.
- *Floods:* The combustion of the comet's hydrogen in the sky causes not only a shortage of oxygen, but also the formation of huge clouds which condense into torrential rains.
- *Hurricanes:* Like the droughts and the floods (both of which will precede and follow the encounter with the comet), the hurricanes are caused by climatic changes. But like the droughts that will *immediately* precede the encounter, and the floods that will *immediately* follow it, the hurricanes also are caused by the encounter itself. Moreover, the huge sky fires will create powerful fire tornadoes. (From this, it follows that there will be at least *three* different waves of droughts, floods, and hurricanes: before, during, and after the encounter — which is what some prophecies say and is in accord with scientific theory.)
- *Darkness:* Caused by the thick dust and gases of the comet's tail and possibly by the thick layers of clouds in the sky following the combustion of the hydrogen and before the torrential rains begin. The sun, then, will be blotted out for three days.
- *Earthquakes and Tidal Waves:* Caused by the gravitational pull of the comet's head.
- *Famines:* Caused by droughts, fires, and floods.
- *Epidemics:* Caused by the famines and injuries.

It is interesting to note, too, that many prophecies mention that the land will yield abundantly during the period of peace which will follow. This is quite understandable: the violent lightning will have enriched the soil with large quantities of nitrogen. Moreover, it is quite possible that some of the dust, which the prophecies say will be released by the comet's tail, will be rich in minerals and have fertilizing properties. The very precipitation of the nitrogen will help restore the proper balance of the atmosphere after the binding of so much oxygen into water. Here, for the benefit of those of my readers who may not be aware of it, I must add that water is a combination of oxygen and hydrogen. The combustion of hydrogen binds some oxygen and produces water. Also, the atmosphere which we breathe is made up of various gases, mainly nitrogen and oxygen. We need oxygen in order to survive. The binding of large quantities of oxygen, therefore, causes asphyxiation. Likewise, lightning precipitates the nitrogen of the air into the soil where it is a fertilizing agent, since all plants need nitrogen, but only a few can absorb it directly from the air. Without this scientific data it would be difficult to understand what has been said above.

3

THE END OF THE WORLD

Christ Himself has warned us that "no one knows of the day and hour, not even the angels of heaven, but the Father only." (*Matt.* 24:36). It is futile, therefore, to attempt to determine any date for the end of the world. At the same time, however, Christ gave us a number of signs to watch for, and he added "When you see all these things, know that it is near, even at the door." (*Matt.* 24:33). Now what are these signs?

1. The Gospel shall be preached in the whole world.
2. A universal falling away from the Faith.
3. The coming of Antichrist.
4. The return of the Jews to the Holy Land.
5. Widespread disturbances of nature.

St. Alphonsus di Liguori enlarges on these signs as follows:

1. The Gospel shall be preached freely in the whole world.
2. All the nations of the earth shall fall away from the Faith.
3. The Holy Roman Empire shall collapse.
4. Antichrist shall come.
5. Henoch and Elias shall return to preach.
6. The Jews shall return to the Holy Land.
7. The powers of heaven shall be shaken.
8. The stars shall fall from heaven.
9. Widespread earthquakes, tidal waves, lightning, wars, famines, and epidemics shall occur.

Now, the question is this: "Have any of these signs come to pass already?" The answer cannot be definite and clear cut. It may be asserted that the first two signs are already here: indeed, the Gospel has been preached in every nation, and there is overwhelming evidence of a general falling away from the Faith. Yet, it has been, and it may still be contended that the preaching of the Gospel must be absolutely world-wide and reach every single human being, and not be merely confined to pockets of missionary activity in every nation. It can also be objected that the current faithlessness is not general enough to be applied to the second sign; indeed, the Church is still very active and influential. Some statesmen are openly professing their Catholic Faith; some governments are wholly or almost wholly Catholic (e.g., Spain, Portugal, and Ireland).

In my opinion, the two interpretations are valid if given the necessary qualifications. This is so because *there are two different stages within the Latter-Days period: the first, heralding the final stage, being of lesser intensity; the final stage bringing about the consummation of the world. To each of these two stages will the proximate signs of the End apply. Thus, we are now about to enter the first stage, the Great Disaster which is imminent and which will be followed by a period of peace.* So, we can already see the signs of its coming: the Gospel has been preached in every nation (although imperfectly), and the falling away from the Faith is worldwide (yet incomplete). Then, the lands of the former Roman Empire will be in a state of utter chaos and anarchy. Communism (a prefiguration of Antichrist) will triumph (but its victory will be as short-lived as that of Antichrist some thirty years later). The Great King to-be and the Holy Pontiff will reveal themselves to the world and fight Communism, thus prefiguring Henoch and Elias. Stones will fall from heaven; earthquakes and tidal waves will wreak havoc throughout the world; famines and epidemics will be widespread. Thus will come the end of the first stage, or "the Good Friday of Christendom." The resurrection will be spectacular: the Great King will be the Emperor of Western Europe, and anointed by the Holy Pontiff. Many Jews and all non-Catholic Christians will turn to the True Faith. The Mohammedans will embrace Christianity, as also the Chinese. In short, virtually the whole world will be Catholic. This universal preaching of the Gospel, in turn, will constitute the first sign of the second stage. Toward the end of the Great King's reign, people will fall away again from the Faith (the second sign). Then, the Holy Roman Empire will collapse (Third sign). Antichrist will come (Fourth sign). Henoch and Elias will be sent down again in order to fight Antichrist (fifth sign). The Jews will return to Palestine (sixth sign). New disturbances of nature will take place (seventh, eighth, and ninth signs).

This personal interpretation of mine is based on my knowledge of a large number of private prophecies, and on extensive and painstaking cross-references and correlations made many years ago, when I was in a position to devote much time to studying these prophecies. Moreover, this interpretation is not incompatible with Scripture. Indeed, Scripture supports it in many cases. We read in the Gospel, for instance, a description of various evils followed by the caution: *"But the end is not yet"* (*Matt.* 24:6), and, again, a description of pestilence, famines and earthquakes, with the conclusion: *"But these things are the beginnings of sorrows,"* (*Matt.* 24:8), the first stage only. Then, we are told that *"the Gospel is to be preached in the whole world"* (*Matt.* 24:14) before the End finally comes. In Verse 15, another description of these events is given, but it is clear that Verses 9 to 14 formed an indivisible whole, as did Verses 4 to 8. Then, at the end of that third passage (Verses 15 to 22) we are informed again that *those days will be shortened for the sake of the elect, otherwise no living creature would be saved.*

For the above reasons I regard it as certain that there will be two different stages. The first stage will only be the beginning of sorrows, and it will be shortened for the sake of the elect, and the Gospel will then be preached throughout the world. This will be the period of peace under the Great Monarch, the period of conversions and general prosperity which we and our children may enjoy — in short, the period of peace promised by Our Lady of Fatima.

4

NOSTRADAMUS

¶ 75. *Michel De Nostredame* (Michael of Our Lady) Known as Nostradamus. Nostradamus was born in the South of France in 1503 where he studied the humanities. He obtained his doctorate in philosophy and medicine at the age of twenty-six. Later, he was appointed adviser and personal physician to the Kings of France, a post which he retained through the reigns of Henry II, Francis II, and Charles IX. A member of the Third Order of St. Francis, he enjoyed the friendship of Pope Pius IV. He was a devout Catholic all his life, and he died in 1566.

I make no apologies for quoting Nostradamus. I am aware, of course, that he is not regarded very highly by some of the more educated people in this part of the world, although he enjoys considerable popularity among lovers of sensationalism. This unfortunate state of affairs has been brought about by the shameless commercial exploitation of his works. In point of fact, however, Nostradamus was an authentic seer and, in the Old World, many an erudite has not deemed it beneath his dignity to spend long hours poring over his predictions. The list of lay and clerical authors who have written books on Nostradamus over the last 150 years is quite impressive, and I once knew a medical specialist of high renown, a man of great learning, now deceased, who wrote at least three books on the prophecies of Nostradamus. His familiarity with the Greek and Latin languages and with the dialect of southern France enabled him to decipher many of the most obscure of Nostradamus' coined words.

Yes, I have every reason indeed to regard Nostradamus as a genuine seer. I know that Dr. Rumble of Sydney would not agree with me, and Dr. Rumble is quite an erudite too — on a par with some of the clerical writers I have just mentioned. But, however great his erudition, Dr. Rumble had to specialize in *breadth* of knowledge rather than in *depth*. This was required by his very functions as a "Radio-Replies" man. No one could possibly answer such diverse questions as he was

asked without having at his disposal a good library of reference books. But once you consult a work of reference, you
have to take at its face value the information given therein.
On controverted questions, this is unreliable.

Although a pygmy compared to the intellectual giant that
Dr. Rumble is, I, on the other hand, became acquainted with
Nostradamus not less than thirty-two years ago and feel en-
titled to say without exaggeration that I know the man and
his works. Not only the man and his works, but also a number
of the works that have been written about him. This necessary
introduction being made, here now are some of his prophecies.

¶ 75.1 4.50

> Libra shall see the Hesperides reign,
> Of heaven and earth shall hold the monarchy,
> Not to perish under any Asian forces,
> Until seven in rank have held the Hierarchy.

Comment: A bad start, you may say! It is unintelligible. Not
really so, however, once you are fully acquainted with Nostradamus' symbolism.

The Hesperides' Gardens is that fabulous land of plenty,
west of Gibraltar, from which Hercules brought back to
Greece the Golden Apples. That land is the United States, and
the above quatrain, interpreted, should read thus:

> Under the sign of Libra, America shall reign,
> Shall hold power in the sky and on land,
> Shall never perish under Asian forces,
> Until seven Pontificates have passed.

Comment: As a great world power, the U.S.A. began its
"reign" during the First World War — but it was not the
greatest world power; in 1918, that was France. In 1945,
however, the U.S.A. was, by and large, the greatest world
power. I think it is from the reign of Pius XII that the seven
Pontificates must be counted, and this brings us to the last
Pope according to St. Malachy's list — when the world will
end. It is debatable, of course, whether the U.S.A. is still the
leading world power; the inane policies of the Washington
politicians since 1945 have been quite successful in lowering
U.S. prestige and influence, and the Vietnam War seems to

suggest that the giant has feet of clay. However, it must be borne in mind that the Washington politicians have never really wanted to win the Vietnam War. That war could have been won within a few months if the U.S. Army had been allowed to land in North Vietnam. Finally, in the unlikely event of an all-out war with Soviet Russia, I am inclined to think that the U.S. would prove the stronger of the two. The greatest weakness of the U.S. is moral corruption. But, miraculously, when an *all-out* war erupts, people pull themselves up by the bootstraps and forget about drugs and sex. On the other hand, the greatest weakness of Soviet Russia is internal discontent, and when a global war breaks out, the dissenters, far from rallying round the Government, may seize this unique opportunity to revolt. We saw this during World War II when whole Russian armies, hundreds of thousands of soldiers, defected to the Germans and were anxious to liberate their homeland under the leadership of their general, Vlassov. To my mind, this is why Soviet Russia is so careful in its dealings with the U.S. They just do not relish the prospect of a global war. And if the Washington political careerists had taken this into account since 1945, it is fairly certain that Communism would now be a thing of the past — without any war. The history of post-war U.S. diplomacy is a story of missed opportunities.

I must be pardoned for elaborating on the subject. But this study in prophecy would lose its significance — in fact might become irrelevant if I did not examine the political context of the period to which these prophecies refer. So, let me explain a little further the story of "missed opportunities."

In 1945, the U.S. was the *only* nuclear power in the world. When the Soviets decided on the Berlin Blockade, what did the U.S. do? At great expense, it organized an air bridge; whereas, the only logical answer worthy of the leading nation was to force the way with tanks through the blockade. No, there would have been no war: the Russians could not afford it. But their loss of prestige in the satellite countries would have been tremendous, and the consequences for them would have been incalculable.

Next came the Korean War. General MacArthur had a plan to finish it quickly, a plan that would have *in the process* brought to its knees the rising power of Communist China. But Washington opposed it and recalled MacArthur (as a reward for his genius, no doubt). In 1956 there was Hungary; after the popular uprising, the Russian tanks left the country and remained poised for several days on the other side of the border, waiting to see what action the U.S. would take. Meantime, the newly-formed Hungarian government asked the U.S. for support — which was refused — and they then approached several European countries. Spain offered to send a few planes, but re-fuelling facilities were required in West Germany. West Germany did grant, or was about to grant, those facilities when the U.S. stepped in and threatened West Germany with economic sanctions. Bonn had to back down. Result, the Russian tanks poured back into Hungary and crushed the uprising in a bloodbath.

Is it the end of the "missed opportunities?" Not in the least! but I cannot review them all: Yalta, Poland, East Germany, the Middle East, Cuba, Laos, Vietnam, Czechoslovakia, the list is long indeed. And, except in these last few years, the risk of all-out war with Russia was non-existent. Even now, this risk is minimal if the Washington politicians would but allow the U.S. Army to show its teeth.

Back now to Nostradamus. He foresaw the Age of Enlightenment and the subequent development of the printed word which man is using to boast of his achievements. It is to be noted that in his time printed books were still comparatively few.

¶ 75.2   Letters will do such great and unequalled boasting . . .

He foresaw the development of radiology and, as his apposition of "rare metals" and "waves" makes clear, the development of nuclear power — a thing which was undreamed of in his time.

¶ 75.3   "The complete transformation of incorruptible metals and mysterious waves. . ." (i.e. Plutonium and Gamma and Beta rays).

He foresaw the decadence of the spiritual and temporal powers (the Church and the secular governments), modern irreligion, and the general revolt against authority; plus, he foresaw that the Church would be affected first. Indeed, it is only within the last twenty years that anarchy has been spreading; whereas, irreligion began in the 18th century.

¶ 75.4 "Momentous and painful events, calamitous adventures are drawing close . . . first, the temples of the Lord; then, those whose power is on earth, when the enemies of Jesus Christ shall begin to multiply. . ."

He also foresaw much of what the other prophecies mention:

¶ 75.5 "I find that learning shall be at a great loss, and that so many great floods shall happen before the universal conflagration, that there shall scarcely be any land that shall not be covered with water, and this shall last so long that except from what lives on mountains and in waters, all shall perish. Before and after these floods, however, there shall be such scarcity of rain and such a great deal of fire, and burning stones shall fall from heaven, that nothing unconsumed shall remain. The world shall be so diminished, and so few men shall be left on earth, that not enough will be found to plow the fields, and these will stay in fallow as long as they had once been tilled."

He gave the correct date when the Christian Calendar was abolished in France: (It was restored later by Napoleon I.)

¶ 75.6 "And it shall be in the year 1792, which will be thought to be a renewal of time. . ."

He foresaw the rise of authoritarian régimes in Italy, Germany and Spain (Mussolini assumed power in 1922, Hitler in 1933, Franco in 1938).

¶ 75.7 "And three regions shall be over a wide extent of leagues, namely, the Roman, the German, and the Spanish. They shall be equal in nature, but much different in faith."

There is another passage that should be inserted before the last sentence above, but it is practically impossible to translate it satisfactorily as the sense is quite obscure. However, it clearly refers to a war, and two or three countries, by indicating the nearest latitude of their capital cities. Thus, 48° for Paris (although it should really be 49°); 50° for Prague; 52° for London, Berlin and Warsaw. It goes on to say that the first areas (50° and 52°) will be the first to "tremble", followed by the Western, the Southern and the Eastern, in that order. Indeed, Prague and Warsaw were the first to "tremble" (March 1939 and September 1939). Then, came Paris (May 1940); Greece (October 1940); Russia (June 1941). It could not have been more accurate. Yet, it is impossible to reconstruct this passage, which is a jumble of verbs, nouns and adjectives, with no apparent connection. This obscurity, of course, is deliberate. In nine different passages at least, Nostradamus explains that it is not expedient to be too specific and that he has "roughed up" his original vaticinations so that they might be passed by the ecclesiastical censor. "But," he says, "I could have given the dates for every event which my prophetical instinct enabled me to see because I have worked out all dates through astrological calculations." Nostradamus had a *natural* gift of clairvoyance coming from God, of course, as all things come from God, but *not* immediately inspired by God. Moreover, he was a scientist and an accomplished scholar. Astrology had no secrets for him, and it is his knowledge of astrology that enabled him to find out the dates (he gives precisions about this in twelve different passages).

Astrology is, to the mind of modern men, a superstition, but it was not so in the past, in those so-called Dark Ages which, in his foolish pride, modern man derides. Astrology was then held in high esteem by men such as Galileo and St. Thomas Aquinas. It is only comparatively recently that rationalistic philosophers and scientists decided that there was nothing but superstition in Astrology (although, to be sure, a great deal of what is currently presented as "Astrology" is just that). Yet, some fifteen years ago in Paris, a group of biologists and radiologists established experimentally that the sun and the moon did influence some biological processes. And since the exercise of our free-will depends on our thinking power, which in turn rests on biological processes, it is not hard to see that the stars may indeed have a bearing on the future of mankind. Let us consider another passage on the Second World War:

¶ 75.8 "Italy, emulating Ancient Rome, will raise great armies and put her wings high in the sky (planes). And at that time, great Byzantine sails (the British fleet based in the

Middle East), with the help and power of Aquila (the American Eagle), shall meet the Ligustics (Italians) and hinder them so, that the two Cretans (the perfidious ones: Hitler and Mussolini), shall not keep their faith. In the sea, there shall be great commotion, beginning in the Panpotam (Sicily) to the European Mesopotamia (Italy) at forty-five and others, from forty-one, forty-two, and thirty-seven."

Comment: This passage would have been incomprehensible *before* the events it describes. But not so now. "Pan-Potam" means Sicily because this coined word means in effect "island". European "Meso-Potamia" means Italy because the word means "Peninsula" in Greek. The figures 45, 41, 42, and 37 are degrees of latitude. And so, this passage can be explicated as follows:

"Italy will emulate Ancient Rome. She will raise great armies and put her planes in the sky. But the British fleet of the Middle East, supported by the Americans, will confront the Italians with the result that Italy and Germany will not keep their faith. There will be great activity at sea. It will begin in Sicily (where he Americans under Patton, and the English under Montgomery landed in July 1943). It will be then carried to the mainland of Italy."

All this is strictly correct: the Anglo-Americans landed in Sicily first (37° of latitude), then on the mainland at Naples and Salerno (Between 41° and 42° latitude) where bloody fighting took place. Finally, the war ended when the Allies had reached the North of Italy (45°). Meantime, and even before the Salerno landing took place, the Italians had broken their faith with Germany (six days before, exactly), so that the Fifth American Army of General Clark was confronted, not by Italian troops, but by German troops under Rommel and Kesselring. Let us now turn to Nostradamus' prophecies of events yet to come.

As the above passage has shown, it is extremely difficult to interpret Nostradamus' predictions *before* the events. Once the events have come to pass, however, some significant details *always* make it possible to identify the passage concerned. Regarding the future, therefore, all one can do is to give an outline, and qualify any possible interpretation of details by means of a question mark.

¶ 75.9 "After this, the Barren Female (the revolution), more powerful than the second (Russian Revolution), shall be received in two countries: the first, obstinate, which used to rule all the others (England?); the second, and the third which shall deploy its forces in Eastern Europe, shall be defeated in Pannonia (Hungary) but shall send its navy to Sicily and to the east coast of Italy before being soundly defeated in Italy and in Germany."

Comment: The "Second" is probably Italy where the Revolution will be raging according to many prophecies. The "Third" will not be in the throes of a revolution; it is the Arab world, "the southern Ally of Russia," as Nostradamus says elsewhere. The Mohammedans will take advantage of the complete anarchy prevailing in Western Europe, and proclaim a new "Holy War." They will be armed by Soviet Russia who will endeavor not to become involved directly, at least not in the beginning.

¶ 75.10 "And in that time and in these countries the Powers of Hell shall set up against the Church of Jesus Christ the might of the enemies of His law. This will be the second Antichrist, and he will persecute the Church and its true Vicar through the power of temporal rulers who, in their ignorance, shall have been deceived by high-sounding words that will do more harm than a sword in the hands of a madman. And this shall last until the appearance of him who is of noble birth and whose time shall have come. . ." [some unintelligible details follow this].

Comment: Here the role of Russia is clearly outlined: no direct involvement, but her propaganda will deceive many foreign rulers, ignorant of the true purpose and nature of Communism. And this will last until the appearance of the Great King to-be. As we have seen earlier, Russia will finally intervene directly but will be defeated by the Great King with the help of God.

Soviet Russia is called the "second Antichrist". In fact, there will be only one Antichrist properly so-called, and he will come at the end of the Great King's reign. But, according to Nostradamus, two others will come before who can be called Antichrist figuratively. The first Antichrist was either Hitler or Napoléon. Let us recall here that Nostradamus calls Napoleon "the first Son of the Revolution." Likewise, he calls the Russian Revolution, the "second" revolution. It seems likely, then, that the first Antichrist was Napoleon who forcibly brought back to France the Popes of his time and cast them into jail (Pius VI and Pius VII). Surely, a temporal ruler who lays his hands on the Vicar of Christ is an Antichrist by that very act.

Note, too, the reference to the "true" Vicar of Christ — which seems to imply that there will be a "false" one, or an anti-pope.

¶ 75.11   "Then shall there be against the Church a greater persecution than ever was. And thereupon such great epidemics shall develop that more than two-thirds of the world shall perish, so much so that no one shall know the owners of the fields and houses, and grass shall grow in the streets of the cities knee-high and even more.

"In those days of desolation the largest cities will be depopulated, and he who would return therein shall be struck by the wrath of God. And the Sacred Place shall be turned into a stable for cattle, large and small, and put to profane uses. O what a calamitous time shall it be for women with child! (Cf. *Matt.* 24:19).

"And during the said astrological computations, in harmony with Holy Writ, the persecution against the clergy shall have its beginning in the power of the North united with the East, and it shall last eleven years, or a little less, when the chief northern ruler shall fall, and his southern ally shall persecute the Church even more for three years by the apostolical seduction of one who has absolute power over the militant Church of God.

"The holy people of God, the keepers of His law, and all the religious orders shall be grievously persecuted and afflicted, so much that the blood of the true ecclesiastics shall flow all over. One of these horrible temporal rulers shall be highly praised by his followers for having spilled more of the innocent ecclesiastics' human blood than anyone could do with wine. The said ruler shall commit incredible crimes against the Church, and human blood shall run in the streets and in the churches as water after a heavy rainstorm. And the rivers shall also be red with blood."

Comment: Here, again, the mention of "true" ecclesiastics seems to imply that a section of the clergy will apostatize and follow the anti-pope. Concerning the "eleven" years, I definitely think that this is a mistake — perhaps a misprint in the original edition. It should read either eleven months, or one year. One and eleven cannot be confused in English, but in old French an extra letter and the substitution of an "o" for a "u" turns one into eleven. A misprint is therefore a distinct possibility. All other prophecies say that the great crisis will be of short duration, and the whole events should not last more than four years.

¶ 75.12   "And the countries, towns, cities, governments, and provinces which had left their former ways in the belief that they would free themselves, but which had become more deeply enslaved by treachery and had lost their religion, shall then start to strike on the left part in order to return to the right, and shall give back to the Church her former glory."

Comment: This passage is plain enough: many nations will choose Communism in the belief that they will thus win complete freedom. This will be achieved by treachery and lying promises. (See previously: "high-sounding words that will do more harm than a sword in the hands of a madman.") But they will realize their error, and a general popular uprising against Communism will take place. They will strike the left to return to the right, and under the leadership of the Great King, they will restore the Church to her former glory. This is a remarkable prophecy, seeing that it was written in the 16th century when neither the right nor the left existed in the political spectrum.

Another lengthy passage follows the above excerpt, but the style is clumsy, and the sentences run for lines on end without a single full stop. Little would be gained by quoting it in full. Here are the salient points with my own interpretation:

¶ 75.13   "The Communists will at first try to deceive (the Christians), but as soon as they think they are masters of the whole world they will know no restraint and will begin to liquidate people by the million. However, a stupendous phenomenon will thwart their plans. (See previous prophecies). Taking advantage of this, a number of military leaders will rebel and will deprive Communism of its "two swords" (Deceit and War), leaving only the symbols of these (the hammer — brutal force; and the sickle — the lies that undermine from below). These symbols will make a last attempt to arouse the people's enthusiasm, but in vain. The Great King to-be will then be known, and the people will follow him in order to free themselves from the slavery they had themselves consented to. They will take up arms, and the uprising will begin in a city astride two rivers (possibly the city of Plancus, mentioned elsewhere, in which case it would be Lyons, in France). Finally, the supreme Communist ruler himself will be unseated and put in the pillory.

¶ 75.14 "Then, within the same year and through the following years, a most horrible epidemic of plague shall break out, caused by the preceding famine, and such great tribulations as never have happened since the foundation of the Christian Church in the Latin regions, not even in Spain where traces remain. Thereupon, the third ruler of Aquila, hearing the cries of anguish of the peoples of his principal title, shall raise up so great an army, and shall retrace the steps of his ancestors in order to put most nations back on their feet again.

"Then, shall the Great Vicar of the Cope be restored in his former estate."

Comment: This is one of the very few references to an American intervention to be found in the prophecies. This intervention will take place toward the end of the holocaust. That this passage refers to America is almost certain. The "title" of the U.S.A. is its being Western and European in culture, even though it lies beyond the ocean. Nostradamus gives the added precision that he "shall retrace the steps of his ancestors." Moreover, the emblem of the American Coat of Arms is the White Eagle (Aquila in Latin). But why the *"third* ruler of Aquila?" The most likely interpretation is that there shall rise a *great* American president, of the stature of George Washington and Abraham Lincoln, who will thus be "the third [*great*] ruler of Aquila." There is a lengthy prophecy about such a person which, as well as I can determine, has never been fulfilled by any one so far. But there is a deliberate ambiguity in Nostradamus' terminology; he uses the word "Aquilonnaire" which may mean either "of Aquila", or "of the North wind". As a result, the word may stand for either "U.S.A." or "Russia", according to the context. But the context, here, makes it clear that Aquila is the U.S.A. To a 16th or even 19th-century reader, however, it would not have been clear by any means; this is one of the characteristics of many prochecies: quite obscure at first, until the developments of history allow for an interpretation. But, in previous passages, I have translated "Aquilonnaires" by "Northern" = Russian, because the context made it clear that it could not possibly mean the U.S.A. This is plain common sense: no one in his right mind will contend that Russia will "help" other nations, or that the U.S.A. will cause the clergy to be slaughtered. Hence, the First, Second and Third Ruler of Aquila: Russia, China, U.S.A., but with an entirely different sense each time.

Concerning the "Great Vicar of the Cope", two interpretations are possible: 1) the Pope will come from a religious order in which a Cope is part of the habit, or 2) he will be a descendant of the Capet family — some prophecies say that he will be of royal blood.

¶ 75.15   "Then, from that stock that has long been barren, proceeding from the 50th degree, one will come who will renew the entire Christian Church. And there shall be great peace, union and harmony between the offsprings of the separated and lost Heads."

Comment: The 50th degree crosses the Ardennes, the cradle of the Capetian family. This prophecy may refer either to the Great King or to the Holy Pontiff — it is impossible to say. The "separated Heads," or leaders, were the schismatics. The "lost Heads" were the heretics. Their descendants will be reunited. This passage has not been quoted in full, and the rest is obscure. One phrase, however, seems to refer to the conversion of Soviet Russia; this, added to the fact that peace will be universal, is in accord with the Fatima prophecy.

¶ 75.16   10.86

As a Griffin the King of Europe shall come,
Accompanied by those of Aquila.
Of Reds and Whites shall lead a great army,

Shall march against the King of Babylon.

The Great King is here represented as a Griffin — a mythical creature formed with the body of a lion, the head and wings of an eagle, and the dorsal fin of a fish. This comparison may be explained by the fact that his will be a motley army, and we have seen that some seers call him the "Lion" or the "Eagle."

The Great King will receive the assistance of the U.S.A. (Aquila). By that time (probably after the victory of Westphalia against the Prusso-Russians) Communism will have been defeated. Many former Communists troops will defect and join the forces of liberation. This union of Reds and Whites will throw back to the sea the invading Mohammedan forces (King of Babylon).

Nostradamus wrote other quatrains on this episode. Following is one in which the Arab Power is called a "mastiff." (We have seen elsewhere that it was called a "dog"). Greatly assisted by Soviet Russia (the Bear), the Arabs will invade Italy (the Wolf) and confirm their alliance there. But as we have seen previously, Communism will eventually collapse, and former Communist troops (whose soldiers are no more Communist than you or I) will join the Great King's forces, to the great displeasure of the Mohammedans. Here is this quatrain:

¶ 75.17 5.4

The Great Mastiff, driven out of the City (Rome),
Shall be annoyed at the strange alliance (of Reds and Whites).
After having pursued the Leader (Pope) in the Fields,

The wolf and bear shall defy each other.

The "fields" mean that the Pope and the Clergy will be forced to go into hiding in the open country, an event which will take place at the beginning of the Great Disaster when Arabs and Reds are still friends.

There is still another quatrain describing the final phase of the Great Disaster:

¶ 75.18 6.21

When those of the Arctic are allied together,
There shall be in the East great fear and great trembling.
One newly elected holding the Great Temple,
Rhodes, Istanbul shall be dyed with barbarian blood.

"When those of the Arctic . . ." means Russia and the U.S.A. We have seen already "North," "North Wind," and "Aquilonnaires" which can be rendered by "Aquila" (Eagle) or "North Wind." Here the U.S.A. is referred to as "Arctic" because of its synonymity with "Aquilonnaires" and also possibly because the U.S. will send its troops and arms over the North Pole. Russia, of course, will no longer be Soviet Russia, but a new Russia allied with the U.S.A. and Western Europe to repel the Mohammedan invasion for which the Soviet government had been responsible. The East may also refer to China, but this is not certain. At that time, a new Pope will have been elected. The Christian forces will cross the seas and annihilate the Arab forces in the Middle East.

Nostradamus' quatrains were deliberately shuffled as one does with a deck of cards. It follows that there is no order in his 1,000 or so quatrains. Yet many correlations can be found, and it may be possible to restore the original order, although this would entail a time-consuming procedure which does not appear to be worthwhile, considering that the succession of events to come is fairly well delineated in the other private prophecies. One need only fit in those quatrains which clearly have a bearing on events already described. That is what I have done here, after having quoted a sufficient number of private prophecies earlier in this book. Following are a few more quatrains which either corroborate or complement what we already know:

¶ 75.19 3.95

> The Moorish law shall be seen to decline,
> Past another that was more seductive,
> The Boristhenes shall be the first to fall,
> Through bribes and words was much more attractive.

This means that Soviet Russia (Boristhenes), despite its bribes and lying propaganda, will collapse *before* the Arab power does, and the latter will not possess the appeal that Communism had. The French did not use "bribes and words," but "gifts and tongues;" but the real sense is that given in my translation.

Many prophecies, and in particular the *Apocalypse,* mention the Beast of the Earth and the Beast of the Sea — the Dragon and the Hydra. No doubt, these apply to the time of Antichrist which is the second phase of the Latter Days, but they also apply to a lesser extent to the first phase. The

Dragon, or first Beast of the Earth, is Soviet Russia. The Hydra, or Beast of the Sea, is the Arab power that will come across the Mediterranean Sea. The Hydra will be powerful because Western Europe will be in chaos and thrown into confusion by the Dragon's work, but especially because Soviet Russia will arm the Arabs, which is exactly what the *Apocalypse* says (13:2): "The Beast of the Sea shall receive its might from the Dragon."

In the same period of time, the Pope will die in exile. A new Pope will be elected in Rome, but the validity of the conclave will be challenged by a number of Cardinals — the Church will then be in an incredible state of internal dissension. Then, the first Mohammedan forces will march into Rome, coming from Albania where they had probably landed, Albania being the only Mohammedan nation in Europe at the present time, and also a Communist country. Here is this quatrain:

¶ 75.20 5.46

> By the Red Hats, quarrels and new schisms,
> When the Sabine shall have been elected.
> Great sophisms against him shall be said,
> And Rome shall be wounded by Albanians.

¶ 75.21 5.47

> The Great Arab shall progress well forward,
> But betrayed shall be by Byzantines. (Turks)
> The ancient Rhodes shall come and shall meet him,
> Then great evil shall befall Hungary.

Here, we are told that Turkey will break its faith with the rest of the Arab world. Turkey, it will be remembered, is the only Mohammedan Power having adopted the Roman alphabet. What the third verse says about Rhodes may mean that the Knights of St. John, who once held Rhodes (1311-1533), will again become powerful and play a dominant role in military affairs. As for the fourth verse, it alludes once again to the determining battles which are to take place in Hungary.

The number of quatrains which Nostradamus has written on the Mohammedan invasion is quite impressive; it does not appear necessary, however, to quote them all. Suffice it to say that the Mohammedans will overrun the whole of Southern Europe. In France, they will be stopped on the banks of the river Loire. In Germany, however, they will cross the Danube, reach the Rhine, and possibly the North Sea. In Eastern Europe they will clash with the Poles who, by then, will have shaken off their Communist yoke. The Mohammedans will commit innumerable atrocities, but no great military feats, since Europe will already be on its knees through civil wars. As soon as the European nations can gather up their forces again, the Mohammedans will suffer crushing defeats on every front, will be thrown back to the sea again, and pursued into their own homelands — which will mark the prelude to their conversion to Christianity.

Below are now a few additional quatrains with a bearing on various events predicted by many seers:

¶ 75.22 2.41 (*The Comet, The Arab "Mastiff", the exile of the Pope*)
> For seven days the great star shall be seen,
> As if two Suns in the sky should appear.
> The big Mastiff shall be howling all night,
> When the Pontiff shall go into exile.

¶ 75.23 2.43 (*The Comet, the earthquakes*)
> During the time the hairy star appears . . .
> Struck from heaven, shaky peace, shaking earth . . .

¶ 75.24 2.18 (*The Rain of Stones*)
> New downpour, sudden, impetuous,
> Unexpected, shall hinder two armies.
> Stone, Heaven, Fire, shall fall over the sea . . .

The suddenness of the natural disasters is noteworthy; it has been stressed by many seers. These acts of God will stop men from killing one another pointlessly. The killing will go on *after* the disturbances of nature have begun, but it seems that it will no longer be *pointless*. Chaos, anarchy, blind hatred will give way to organized fighting against the two Beasts. At any event, these disasters will mark the turning of the tide; from then onwards the enemies of God will suffer nothing but defeat. In a somewhat elliptic and symbolic form, the following verses lay stress on this particularity: The leaders of men will be overcome by the forces of the Infinite when the stones hidden in the "hair" of the comet start falling. Then the leaders will vainly attempt to enforce their rulings, but death will deprive them of any effective means. Here it is:

¶ 75.25 2.47

> The sovereigns by Infinite conquered,
> Stones are raining, hidden under the hair,
> Through death in vain shall rulings be invoked.

Many more quatrains describe the passage of the comet, the three days of darkness, and the accompanying disasters including the fiery rain of stones. This, said Nostradamus, is to take place late in March and early in April.

Once more, Nostradamus mentions the American intervention. Of all the prophecies I possess, Nostradamus is the most explicit in this respect:

¶ 75.26 4.39

> The Rodians shall ask for assistance,
> Forsaken by neglect of their sons.
> Arab Empire shall roll back in its course,
> By Hesperides the cause shall be restored.

The Rodians, as stated above, may well mean the Knights of St. John, who, as prominent champions of Christian civilization once more, in dire straits because its members failed to respond to a call to arms, may invoke their influence with the American government and request American assistance. The Americans will come, and things will be straightened out.

That the Americans will finally intervene is beyond doubt. In this case, however, the above interpretation is not absolutely certain. Nostradamus often uses the same word for different things. In some quatrains, it is clear that "Hesperides" means America. In the above quatrain, it may just mean any land west of Gibraltar, in which case it could be Portugal. What prompts me to this word of caution is the following quatrain.

¶ 75.27 6.85

> Great city of Tarsus by Gauls shall be destroyed,
> All those wearing turbans shall be made prisoners,
> Through assistance by sea from the great Portuguese,
> The first day of summer when Urban is installed.

This seems to mean that the French, with the help of the Portuguese, will win a battle at Tarsus ("great" equals "famous"; it was St. Paul's birth-place). This will be in June when a new Pope is installed.

Here is now part of the quatrain referring to the new capital of France:

¶ 75.28 3.93

> In Avignon the Head of the Empire (Great King)
> Shall make ready, for Paris desolate . . .

I feel I must now bring to a close these specimens of Nostradamus' extraordinary insights. This does not mean, however, that there is nothing further to be said; far from it, for I could not do justice to Nostradamus even if I were to write a 600-page book. But such a book would involve a tremendous amount of preparation — which is probably why no one has ever attempted it. There is no doubt that, with a certain method of approach, the totality or the near totality of his often obscure quatrains could be understood. The future, then, would be like an open book. Moreover, some definite dates, or some alternative dates, could be given. This is so because Nostradamus, apart from his prophetical instinct and extensive knowledge in many fields, was well versed in astronomy and astrology, two sciences which, it must be remembered, were one and the same in the 16th century.

Nostradamus, therefore, gives many configurations in his quatrains. When these configurations are exceptional and happen, say, once in twenty or thirty years, a definite date could be ascribed to certain events. When they are common and happen, say, every year or so, a number of alternative dates could be given. Some of these alternative dates, in turn, could be eliminated after a careful screening of correlations.

Take for instance the Comet; it is mentioned in many quatrains, but for the sake of simplicity let us imagine that it is mentioned in only two quatrains. *Suppose* the first gives three alternative dates; for instance, 1970, 1973, 1977. *Suppose* further that the second quatrain gives three more alternative dates; for instance, 1973, 1976 and 1979. Since the event is the same, i.e., the Comet, it is obvious that the correct date is that which is common to both quatrains, namely, 1973; and the others can be eliminated.

The elimination of alternative dates could be effected in another way too. For instance, we know that the Great King will fight the Mohammedans. So, we have two different events here: 1) the rise of the Great King, 2) the Mohammedan invasion, but they both happen at the same time. *Suppose* then that the configuration given in respect to the Great King occurs in 1976, 1978, 1980, and the configuration in respect to the Mohammedans in 1978, 1982 and 1984. Well, quite clearly, since these events are simultaneous, the date to be retained is 1978.

In practice, however, it is not so simple as that. For one thing, a configuration may be given for an event which is not easy to understand. Consider for instance:

¶ 75.29 2.35

> In two dwellings at night the fire shall take,
> Many inside shall choke and roast to death,
> Near two rivers for sure it shall happen,
> Sol, Arc, Caper, they shall all lose their lives.

The astronomical data here is that the sun will be in the signs of Sagittarius and Capricorn. This "sky" is not very specific in itself, but we are not concerned with this at the moment; we are concerned with the particular event that will take place then, and we do not really know what it is. How are we going to identify it?

Let us consider the elements of information at our disposal: *Two dwellings, at night, fire, many inside will die, two rivers.* Our next step will be a quest for correlations; we are going to go through the 1,000 quatrains and look for those which contain one or several of the above elements of information. Then, we will determine whether a relationship really exists, and if so, we shall know what it is all about. But it is hardly necessary to point out how time-consuming such a job would be!

If the same is to be done with every quatrain, it will take quite a few years, although towards the end, we should know most of the quatrains by heart. There is really only one way to tackle the problem satisfactorily: feed all the elements of information into a computer, and it will sort them out on demand within a few seconds. Supposing we find an average of five elements in each quatrain, we shall have 5,000 elements to feed into the computer. Not very many, you may say. In fact we will get many more. This is so because it is not sufficient to feed individual words, but rather all the different meanings that a given word may assume.

It is impossible, then, to estimate the number of elements we should finally obtain. Nevertheless, the task is quite feasible with the help of a computer. It remains only to be seen whether it is really worth the trouble, and I do not think it is. To satisfy our curiosity has never been the purpose of the prophecies, but only to warn, enlighten, and comfort. And what we now possess is quite sufficient to fulfill this function.

We have been warned that an apocalyptic disaster is about to come; we have been enlightened because those prophecies tell us that practically all the values cherished by the modern world — social, political, and philosophical — are erroneous and deadly. We live in fact in an abyss of errors, a bottomless pit of fallacies. Finally, we have been comforted because these prophecies tell us that a wonderful period of peace will follow and a unique Church revival; we know for certain, therefore, that the forces of evil in general and Communism in particular *shall not prevail.*

This gives us hope and courage. We must fight on, and we shall fight on. Those who do not believe, however, are deprived of such hope and certainty, and since on the face of it, the victory of Communism seems inevitable, these people have no alternative but to seek compromises every time they can. That is what politicians have been doing for many decades, thus furthering the cause of Communism, and that is what the Catholic Church Hierarchy — which at the present time scorns private prophecies — has started to do with that sorry business called "dialogue."

5

THE PRESENT STATE OF THE CHURCH

The Church is indeed in a sorry state, and this can no doubt be ascribed to the crisis of discipline which has affected the hierarchy, the clergy, and the laity alike. Indeed, a crisis of discipline is bound to bring in its train a crisis of faith and a crisis of morals, the ravages of which are so glaringly evident today that no elaboration is necessary here.

The point to bear in mind, if one is to steer clear of the many pitfalls which surround every Catholic, is that the current crisis was predicted long ago, and not only predicted, but also described in some detail, so that we might recognize it when it came, and also the circumstances obtaining in the world at the time of the crisis. In this connection it must be remembered that the Great Chastisement is to *follow* the crisis. Any mention of the Great Chastisement, therefore, forms part of the circumstances surrounding the crisis.

¶ 76. *Mother Shipton* (16th century). "The great chastisement will come when carriages go without horses and many accidents fill the world with woe. It will come when 'thoughts are flying round the earth in the twinkling of an eye' [i.e. radio-communications], when long tunnels are made for horseless machines, when men can fly in the air and ride under the sea, when ships are wholly made of metal, when fire and water 'great marvels do' [i.e. the steam engine], when even the poor can read books, when many taxes are levied for war."

¶ 77. *Bl. Rembordt* (18th century). "God will punish the world when men have devised marvellous inventions that will lead them to forgetting God. They will have horseless carriages, and they will fly like the birds. But they will laugh at the idea of God, thinking that they are 'very clever.' There will be signs from heaven, but men, in their pride, will laugh them off. Men will indulge in voluptuousness, and lewd fashions will be seen."

¶ 78. *Trappistine Nun of Notre Dame des Gardes.* "Chastisement will come when a very large number of bad books have been spread."

¶ 79. *Abbe Voclin.* "People will speak only of money. Horrible books will be freely available. Intellectuals will argue fiercely among themselves. Then the war will break out that will see the rise of the Great Monarch."

¶ 80. *Jasper.* "When men indulge in sensuous pleasures and voluptuousness, when no one wishes to obey any more, when there is widespread discontent among the peoples of the earth, then Russia will pour out masses of soldiers, and they will reach the Rhine."

¶ 81. *Ven. Anne de la Foi.* "There will be discord within the Catholic Church. In those days, men will wear women's clothes, and women will put on men's clothes."

¶ 82. *M. Porsat* (19th century). "There will be confusion among the clergy."

¶ 83. *Quoted by Abbe Curicque* (19th century). "What caught my attention repeatedly is that a large number of priests will join in the revolution."

¶ 84. *St. Thomas' Apocalypse—Apocrapha* (1st century). "Every man shall speak that which pleaseth him, and my priests shall not have peace among themselves but shall sacrifice unto me with deceitful minds. Then shall the priests behold the people departing from the House of the Lord and turning unto the world. The House of the Lord shall be desolate and her altars will be abhorred. The place of holiness shall be corrupted, and the priesthood polluted."

¶ 85. *Holzhauser* (17th century). "The Great Monarch will come when the Latin Church is desolated, humiliated, and afflicted with many heresies . . . The Mohammedans will come again." (Note: "The *Latin* Church," which presumably, excludes the Eastern-Rite Churches.)

¶ 86. *Bl. Rembordt* (18th century). "These things will come when they try to set up a new kingdom of Christ from which the true faith will be banished."

¶ 87. *Oba Prophecy.* "It will come when the Church authorities issue directives to promote a new cult, when priests are forbidden to celebrate in any other, when the higher positions in the Church are given to perjurers and hypocrites, when only the renegades are admitted to occupy those positions."

We live in an age of revolution and contestation. Never before have priests taken an active part in revolutionary movements; never before have the Church authorities imposed a new liturgy and forbidden the traditional liturgy.

The traditional liturgy, it must be recalled, goes back to apostolic times, and its definitive form was codified by Pope St. Pius V, who, in his Bull *Quo Primum*, gave it force of law *until the end of time*. The New Missal, however, was deviously introduced, arbitrarily imposed, and the Bull *Quo Primum* (which St. Pius V forbade to be abrogated) was quietly dropped from the opening pages of the official Altar Missal.

The New Mass was opposed by the Synod of Bishops in 1967, but some Vatican Officials, in contempt of the will of the bishops, and enlisting the help of six non-Catholic ministers, went ahead with the final version of their work. (The non-Catholic ministers were Dr. George, Canon Jasper, Dr. Shephard, Dr. Konneth, Dr. Smith, and Br. Thurian, representing the World Council of Churches, the Church of England, the Lutheran Church, and the Protestant community of Taize. Their photograph was published in Issue No. 20 of *World Trends.*) With devilish cleverness, they stopped just short of outright heresy, and abusing the trust which their position entailed, they prevailed upon Pope Paul to ratify it.

The New Missal is indeed a radical attack on our Faith. It will destroy the Mass more effectively than Luther's brutal efforts. Having destroyed the Mass, it will inevitably destroy the Church. Having destroyed the Church, it will—inevitably again—destroy the world. For when the blood of Christ is no longer offered on the Altars of our churches, then the blood of men will have to be spilled on the asphalt of our streets.

To discuss the validity or invalidity of the New Mass is

not within the scope of this book. The debate has been raging since 1969 and, while the majority of bishops and cardinals do not question the validity of the Consecration in the new rite, there are a few who have expressed serious misgivings. It is not outside the scope of this book, however, to cite prophecies which have a bearing on the matter:

¶ 88. *Anna-Katarina Emmerick* (19th century). "I saw again the new and odd-looking Church which they were trying to build. There was nothing holy about it . . . People were kneading bread in the crypt below . . . but it would not rise, nor did they receive the body of Our Lord, but only bread. Those who were in error, through no fault of their own, and who piously and ardently longed for the Body of Jesus were spiritually consoled, but not by their communion. Then, my Guide [Jesus] said: 'THIS IS BABEL.' [The Mass in many languages]." (This prophecy was made *circa* 1820 by Anna Katarina Emmerick, a stigmatized Augustinian nun and is recorded in *The Life of Anne Catherine Emmerich* by Rev. Carl E. Schmoeger, C.SS.R., first published in English in 1870 and reprinted in 1968 by Maria Regina Guild, Los Angeles, California.)

The New Missal is an ominous sign of the destruction to come, and these dire forebodings are in complete accord with what the prophecies say, and which can be paraphrased thus: "They wanted to make a new Church, a Church of human manufacture, but God had other designs. The false Church shall be destroyed, and the enemy shall overcome Rome. The pastors shall be scattered, persecuted, tortured, and murdered. The Holy Father shall have to leave Rome, and he shall die a cruel death. An anti-pope shall be set up in Rome."

Such a tragedy would not be permitted by Christ, save as a punishment for the Church's sins. As long as the Church remains sound, the world is comparatively safe. But let the Church be subverted, and the whole world will be plunged into a bloodbath. In the 15th century, the Church's great sin was immorality, but Faith was alive. Then came the Reformation, and the wars of religion. Today, however, the Church's sin is even greater because it is a sin against the first of the cardinal virtues, namely Faith. The punishment must needs be commensurate. The latest and most significant contribution to the process leading up to this is the New Missal, a *pre-heretical* rite, which has made the Mass as changeable as the passing fashions of the world.

Are we then to relinquish all hope and yield to despair? Not in the least! The prophecies give us a warning, but they also give us a promise. They tell us that the Church will prevail and be more resplendent than ever. A wise and holy Pope will restore all things, and he will be revered by the rulers of nations. Peace, prosperity, and happiness will be given to the whole world.

Hope, therefore, not despair, should fill our hearts.

Melbourne, March 1, 1970*

*The last chapter revised and brought up to date in January, 1973.

ALPHABETICAL INDEX

The first numbers preceded by the symbol ¶ are paragraph numbers. The second numbers refer to the Bibliographical Index and are between brackets.

Wallraff, Helen. ¶ 67, (30, 31).
Werdin D'Otrante. ¶ 57, (30, 31).
Wittman, Bishop George. ¶ 68, (30).

BIBLIOGRAPHICAL INDEX

1. *Malédictions et Bénédictions*. J. Gonthier. Paris. Librairie du Carmel. 1963.
2. *Demain*. Baron de Novaye. Paris. P. Lethielleux. 1934.*
3. *Le Monde en Feu*. J. Johannis. Paris. 1936.*
4. *Le Bienheureux Barthélémy Holzhauser*. Canon de Wuilleret.*
5. *La Vie de Sainte Marguerite-Marie*. Fr. A. Hamon, S.J.*
6. *Les Prophéties des Derniers Temps*. Suzzane Jacquemin. Paris, La Colombe. 1958.
7. *Wife, Mother and Mystic*. Rev. Albert Bessieres, S.J. London. Sands & Co., Ltd. 1952.
8. *Fàtima-Merveille du XX° Siècle*. Canon C. Barthas. Toulouse. Fatima Éditions. 1957.
9. *Le Monde de Demain Vu par les Prophètes d' Aujourd'hui*. Albert Marty. Paris. Nouvelles Editions Latines. 1962.
10. *Prophecy For Today*. Edward Connor. Fresno. Academy Library Guild. 1956.
11. *Les Derniers Jours des Derniers Temps*. Dupont-Fournieux. Paris. La Colombe. 1959.
12. *Signes et Messages pour notre Temps*. R. Christoflour. Paris. Buchet-Chastel. Corrêa. 1958.
13. *Recent Apparitions Of The Blessed Virgin Mary*. Stephen Breen. Chicago. Lumen Books. 1953.
14. *By The Queen's Command*, Lawrence F. Harvey. Glasgow. John S. Burns & Sons. 1953.
15. *Russia Will Be Converted*. John M. Haffert. Washington, New Jersey. Ave Maria Institute. 1956.
16. *Light on the Mountain*. John S. Kennedy. New York. Doubleday Image Books. 1956.
17. *Vie de Mélanie—Bergère de la Salette*. (Autobiography presented by Léon Bloy). Paris. Mercure de France. 1954. (Reprinting).
18. *The Woman Shall Conquer*. Don Sharkey. New York. All Saints Press, Inc. 1954.

19. *Les Apparitions de la Sante-Vierge*. J. Goubert et I
    Cristiani. Paris. La Colombe. 1952.
20. *Nostradamus*. James Laver. Harmondsworth. Pengui
    Books. 1952.
21. *L'Étrange XX° Siècle vu par Nostradamus*. Dr. de Font
    brune. Sarlat. Michelet. 1946.
22. *Michel Nostradamus*. M. P. Edouard et Jean Mézerette
    Paris. Belles Editions. 1947.
23. *Les Prophéties de Maistre Michel Nostradamus*. Dr. d
    Fontbrune. Sarlat. Michelet. 1946.
24. *Nostradamus—Ses Propheties*. Emile Ruir. Paris. Edition
    Médicis. 1948.
25. *Les Prophéties pour les Temps Actuels*. Georges Vouloir
    Paris. Éditions Médicis. 1948.
26. *L'Apparition de la Très-Sainte Vierge sur la Montagne
    de la Salette*. (An account given by Mélanie Calvat her
    self, first published in 1879 with the *Imprimatur* of the
    Bishop of Lecce, Count Zola, and reprinted in Montpel
    lier in 1925).
27. *Berthe Petit et la Dévotion au Coeur Douloureux et Im
    maculé de Marie*. G. Canova. Bourg Saint-Maurice
    Oeuvre de Diffusion Mariale. 1946.
28. *De la Salette à Bonate*. (As above). 1947.
29. *Vie d'Anne-Catherine Emmerich*. Rev. K. E. Schmoger
    C.SS.R., translated from the German by Rev. E. de Caza-
    lès, Vicar General and Canon of Versailles. Paris. Li
    brairie P. Téqui. 1950.
30. *The Prophets and Our Times*. R. Gerald Culleton. Fresno
    Academy Duplicating Service. Fresno. 1950.
31. *L'Apocalypse à l'Aide des Prophéties Modernes*. Rev. A.
    de Larminat. (Unpublished Manuscript)**
32. *Voice of Fatima*. (An Australian newspaper).
33. *Pro Manuscripto Book*. Published by J. Jongen. Eisden
    1959.
    New Testament quotations come from the Revision of the
    Challoner-Rheims Version, published in 1950 in New
    York by the Catholic Book Publishing Co.
* Number 2, 3, 4 and 5 are important books quoted by J.
  Gonthier, No. 1, but bibliographical particulars are incomplete.
**This work, together with supplements, comprises more than
  1,000 pages. It is the most complete work of reference on

prophecies that has come to my knowledge. It was compiled after consulting *all* the prophetical books kept at the Bibliothèque Nationale of Paris (The French National Library). It also gives extensive bibliographical references.

CHRONOLOGICAL INDEX

PARAGRAPH INDEX

If you have enjoyed this book, consider making your next selection from among the following . . .